D1284915

The
Death
of the
Mythic God

Other books by Jim Marion

Putting on the Mind of Christ

The

Death

of the

Mythic God

———

THE RISE OF EVOLUTIONARY SPIRITUALITY

JIM MARION

HAMPTON ROADS
PUBLISHING COMPANY, INC.

Copyright © 2004
by Jim Marion
All rights reserved, including the right to reproduce this
work in any form whatsoever, without permission
in writing from the publisher, except for brief passages
in connection with a review.

Cover design by Grace Pedalino
Cover photograph © 2004 Punchstock

Hampton Roads Publishing Company, Inc.
1125 Stoney Ridge Road
Charlottesville, VA 22902

434-296-2772
fax: 434-296-5096
e-mail: hrpc@hrpub.com
www.hrpub.com

If you are unable to order this book from your local
bookseller, you may order directly from the publisher.
Call 1-800-766-8009, toll-free.

Library of Congress Cataloging-in-Publication Data

Marion, Jim, 1945-
  Death of the mythic God : the rise of evolutionary spirituality / Jim
Marion.
       p. cm.
  Includes bibliographical references and index.
  ISBN 1-57174-406-1 (alk. paper)
  1. Spirituality. I. Title.
  BL624.M3465 2004
  204--dc22

                                        2004007722

                 10 9 8 7 6 5 4 3 2 1

          Printed on acid-free paper in Canada

Dedication

This book is dedicated to the Divine Mother and to her two
passionate devotees Andrew Harvey and Eryk Hanut, spiritual
partners and lovers of extraordinary courage and wisdom.

For we know that, up until the present time, all of Creation groans in pain like the pain of childbirth. All of Creation waits with eager longing for God to reveal his children.

—Romans 8:22,19

Contents

Foreword

As human beings, we are conversion machines, converting vision into form. In *Death of the Mythic God* Jim Marion reveals himself as a master spiritual mechanic. He lays out the stepping stones that have taken us into the more advanced spiritual level of consciousness that is now emerging and assembles them in a way that makes it possible for us to arrive personally at this advanced dimension.

In every profession today there are those of the avant-garde who are pointing out the surfacing of a new evolutionary level of consciousness. In the language of their particular areas of expertise they are noting similar advances in consciousness. All, in their own way, are stating that it is now possible to end superstition and close the gap between fact and fiction or cause and effect. Through erudite and empirically substantiated intellectual analysis combined with a highly evolved intuitive spirituality, Marion reconciles our divinity with our humanity, metaphysics with mysticism, the infinite with the finite, and the invisible with the visible.

This book becomes more than a literary achievement. It is a bridge that will doubtless be a blessing for all who cross it. Without judging the present level of consciousness, Jim Marion lays a foundation for those who must have logical explanations for the appropriateness of each stage of our religious or spiritual evolution. He gives us the building blocks that can lead us to an intuitive experience of our individual souls. In a day when to be authentic we must share our humanity as well as our divinity, Jim Marion relates his personal experience as well as offers his accumulated spiritual knowledge.

Given his position as a lawyer practicing in Washington, D.C.'s pressure cooker ambiance, his writing carries conviction precisely because he has been tested at every level. Rather than contradicting age-old scriptures, his examples fulfill them in terms of today's experience. "For he taught them as one having authority, and not as the scribes" can be said of Jim Marion.

—Walter Starcke, member of the Board of Directors
of the Unity Churches, and author of
It's All God and several other books

Acknowledgments

First, I want to thank my editors, Frank DeMarco and Richard Leviton, and all the other wonderful people at Hampton Roads Publishing. Their tireless dedication to bringing out contemporary works of the Spirit to meet the needs of today's seekers is much appreciated, as has been their wonderful assistance to me.

I also want to thank the readers of *Putting on the Mind of Christ*. The responses I have gotten by letter, phone, and e-mail from hundreds of people all over the world who are sincerely dedicated to the spiritual path to higher consciousness have been most gratifying. To receive the heartfelt thanks of readers is an author's greatest blessing.

Third, I would like to thank Ken Wilber, Walter Starcke, Andrew Harvey, Beatrice Bruteau, and Fr. Thomas Keating, OCSO, for their friendship, support, encouragement, stimulation, and love. To be accepted and loved by such great lovers of the Mystic Christ and His Divine Mother has been for me the source of abundant joy.

Finally, I would like to thank the churches and church groups—Unity, Methodist, Presbyterian, Catholic, Metaphysical, Episcopalian, Metropolitan Community, and others—that have held workshops to discuss *Putting on the Mind of Christ* and/or invited me to speak, welcomed me, supported me, and given me the chance to interact with many hundreds of people who are serious about the path to the Divine. May God bless you all in your work and on your paths.

Introduction

Today the entire world is caught up, in one way or another, in what President George W. Bush calls the "war against terrorism." Mr. Bush has asserted that civilization itself is gravely threatened by those who would seek to use terrorism and other forms of violence to disrupt the lives of those with whom they disagree. The events of 9-11-2001 and, since then, the bombings in Bali, Istanbul, Madrid, and elsewhere certainly have shown that terrorists, left unchecked, are determined to wreak havoc among people and nations all over the globe.

In addition, it seems that the whole of Western society, especially in the United States, is wracked by what some have called a "culture war." Millions of citizens are politically aligned against each other on issues such as abortion, women's and gay rights, racial affirmative action, the scientific use of fetal tissue, environmental policies, and many other issues.

Nor has the Christian Church (Protestant, Catholic, and Orthodox), for centuries the dominant religious institution in the West, escaped these culture wars. Entire Christian denominations are threatened with schism over the issues of gay marriage and gay church leaders. There is mass confusion and argument over both new issues of morality, such as cloning and bioengineering, and issues long believed settled, such as the morality of war.

In addition, there are even issues that touch on the core beliefs of the Christian tradition. Many Christians are questioning the credibility of the basic Christian myth—that the Son of God came down from heaven to Earth to save us from sin by dying on a cross. Many are even questioning the very existence of God. All this has resulted in a profound spiritual crisis throughout the West, a crisis compounded by moral scandals in some parts of the Church.

Both the war on terrorism and the culture war, I would argue, reflect the same spiritual crisis. Both are primarily a clash between people whose human consciousness is stuck at the mythic level of consciousness and those whose consciousness has moved beyond the mythic to rational consciousness or even higher. It may come as a surprise to some that there are different levels of human consciousness. I believe, however, that psychology and consciousness studies over the last half-century have now conclusively shown this to be the case. People do not simply disagree about issues. People at different levels of consciousness actually see the world differently. They have different values. They have different moral codes. They behave differently.

The levels of consciousness, moreover, are arranged in a hierarchy. As people mature psychologically and spiritually, they naturally grow from one level of consciousness to the next. People all over the world and in every religion grow step by step through one level of consciousness at a time. Each level serves as the foundation for the next level. For example, the archaic consciousness of infants gives way to the magical consciousness of children. Magical consciousness, in turn, gives way to the mythic consciousness with which I am so concerned in this book. If a person continues to grow spiritually, mythic consciousness gives way to rational consciousness and the levels of consciousness that follow the rational level.

People at the mythic level of consciousness are popularly called fundamentalists. They exist all over the world and in every religion or quasi-religion such as Marxist Communism. I will go into much greater detail in describing mythic consciousness in the early pages of the book, but for now I will merely say that people with mythic consciousness tend to believe that their religion, their ethnic group, their nation, their morality, their values are supreme. They believe that their particular scripture, for example the Bible or the Koran, was uniquely revealed by God and is to be followed literally and exactly even centuries after the revelation even though that revelation was made through men and women whose culture and world views were vastly different from our own.

They believe that God, the mythic God, is a being who is separate from us, lives in the sky (heaven), and intervenes in human affairs whenever believers petition him to do so (God is almost always a "him"). They believe in the literal truth of the myths of their religion (for example, God created the world in six calendar days; Mohammed literally ascended into heaven from the site in Jerusalem marked by the Dome of the Rock; Jesus, unlike other humans, was born in a miraculous manner that left his mother a physical virgin). They see themselves as good and unbelievers as evil. They seek to use the power of the state to impose their beliefs upon unbelievers. They believe that God is on their side and that they are charged with converting the entire world to their beliefs, even if they have to use force to do so.

Both the war on terrorism and the culture wars are primarily clashes between fundamentalists and people who have moved beyond mythic consciousness. Just as hydrogen and oxygen, two gases, combine to make water, a substance with entirely new properties, so too do transformations in human consciousness from one level to the next produce entirely new ways of looking at the world.

People at the rational level of consciousness and above see the world as one. They believe all people are created equal and have inalienable rights such as the right to practice their own religion. They see the world as governed by universal scientific and spiritual laws that apply to everyone no matter what their politics or religion. Thus they usually tolerate fundamentalists even though the favor is normally not returned.

Generally, people at the rational level of consciousness or above do not believe in using force against others unless those others pose a danger to themselves or society. Generally, too, they see men and women as equals and oppose slavery, racial discrimination, and other forms of oppression of some by others. At the rational level of consciousness, they may or may not believe anymore in the mythic sky God who is separate from humans and who intervenes in human affairs (this book explores this matter further). They may therefore be secular or religious depending upon their level of awareness. These are the people who are now clashing with fundamentalists all over the globe and with violent fundamentalists in particular.

In part 1 of this book I examine how the West (and lately the whole world) has come into this profound spiritual crisis. I spell out how, with the rise of rational consciousness (including modern science), belief in the mythic Sky God and the worldview of mythic-level consciousness have declined in the West in the past five hundred years. I examine how the mythic God became ill, and how and why, for millions of Christians, the mythic God is now dead. I will argue that the mythic Sky God was never real. It was only a concept of God that has now become outdated. I will show that even Jesus, two thousand years ago, did not believe in a mythic Sky God. Finally, I will suggest, just as Jesus did, that the real God is within the human heart, not in the sky.

In part 2 of the book I argue that the mythic God and the mythic worldview are now being replaced by evolutionary spirituality. More and more people are seeking the God within themselves. More and more people, especially the young, are calling themselves spiritual and are interested in growing spiritually but are not necessarily interested in organized religion. More and more people are realizing that God or Spirit is that which operates within the world and our hearts as the engine of evolution. God "grows us" from within unto higher and higher levels of consciousness. God actually unfolds in evolution—both collective and individual—without ever having to intervene supernaturally from the outside.

More people are also discovering the levels of human consciousness and are realizing that to grow spiritually they must expand their consciousness, thus following the path of Jesus and the mystics of all the world's great spiritual traditions.

I discuss the various levels of human consciousness, describe where the mass consciousness is today, and give some pointers toward the evolution of consciousness in the near future.

If you are concerned about the state of today's world, about the wars against terrorism and the culture wars, I hope this book gives you a better understanding of the spiritual forces producing these conflicts. If you are concerned about the existence or nonexistence of God, I hope this book gives you a better understanding of how to think about God and shows you why we must now think differently from the way we did in the past. If you are concerned with your own level of inner development, I hope this book assists you on your path, for it is primarily on behalf of the spiritual evolution of the reader that this book is lovingly offered.

Washington, D.C., January 15, 2004

Part I

The Death of God

Introduction to Part I

Over the last hundred years, psychologists and other students of human consciousness have shown that the consciousness of human beings evolves upward from one level to the next, beginning with the archaic consciousness of infants all the way up to the Christ Consciousness and nondual consciousness demonstrated by Jesus. Each level of consciousness has its own "worldview"—that is, people at that level of consciousness see and understand the world in a specific way, one that is distinct from the level of consciousness below them and from the level of consciousness above them.

Beginning with the magical level of small children, each worldview has a different understanding of what is meant by "God." Moreover, each new level of consciousness is less materialistic, less mired or stuck in matter, more spiritual, than the preceding level. As humans progress up the levels, we also become less and less egocentric and narcissistic. We grow step by step in our ability to care for and be compassionate toward others—we grow in our capacity to love. We also grow in responsibility, taking more personal responsibility for our thoughts, words, actions, and omissions.

Not only do individuals evolve in consciousness, but ever so slowly the whole race evolves in consciousness. Following are some of the key ideas about individual and cultural consciousness development.

An infant's consciousness is *archaic,* a primarily physical (and later emotional) level of consciousness, ruled by sensations and impulses. The infant's consciousness is at first so attached to physical matter that the infant is unable to distinguish between its own physical body and its mother's. The infant thinks, in effect, that it is the center of the universe and that all things are connected to itself. Freud called this view of the world "primary narcissism."[1] The infant's first spiritual task is to realize that, much as it may wish to be the center of the universe (so the entire world will respond automatically to its every cry), it is distinct from other beings and objects.

Archaic consciousness was probably the average and dominant worldview of Stone Age peoples. These ancient ancestors of ours *felt* themselves to be part of nature and lived accordingly. They lived primarily by sensation and instinct, and their connection to nature was an immediate sensory and emotional experience.

At age two, the infant's mind begins to emerge as something separate from its physical and emotional being. The child then develops a *magical* consciousness, a type of consciousness in which the child often cannot distinguish between its inner symbolic world and the world of external reality. The child's inner world is a polytheistic Disneyland, full of angels, bogeymen, Santa Claus, and talking animals, and all of these are projections of aspects of the child's own psyche. Onto the fairy godmother, for example, children project the love they have toward the "good" aspects of their mothers. Onto the wicked step-mother are projected their feelings for their "bad" mothers.

Children think of everything in terms of their own "I." When they play hide-and-seek, they think that because they cannot see you (their heads being hidden) you cannot see them (even though their legs are sticking out from their hiding place). Magical consciousness is unable to distinguish between one's own viewpoint and the viewpoint of others. Those in magical consciousness also believe in magic words. They may think that if they chant "rain, rain, go away," the rain will cease. They see everything from their own egocentric point of view.

In terms of moral development, children learn what is considered good and bad or right and wrong in their particular culture or society. But this is not the learning of moral principles or laws. It is purely a matter of reward and punishment, what makes Mommy and Daddy happy and what makes them angry or disappointed.

Gradually, children begin to realize that their own point of view is not all there is.

They realize that magic words don't stop the rain, that hiding one's head is not enough. They begin to appreciate that there are other points of view besides their own. Their self-centeredness lessens. They learn to share, for example.

At the cultural level, magical consciousness is the average and dominant consciousness of most tribal cultures. Such cultures are based upon physical (blood) relationship. Nonrelated tribes are usually seen as enemies. Tribes are polytheistic. They see the sky, thunder, sun, moon, Earth, and other natural phenomena as alive, as gods, and have the religious belief that these natural phenomena can be controlled (in one's favor) by magic words and ceremonies. Just as with modern children at the magical level, all these gods, psychologically, are projections into the environment of aspects of the tribal peoples' own inner psyches. Individuals can be sacrificed to these gods for the good of the tribe, for example, at annual fertility festivals. This was the level of consciousness of most of the world described in the oldest parts of the Bible.

Next we come to *mythic* consciousness. In today's children, mythic consciousness develops about the age of seven, the age that the Church has traditionally called "the age of reason," when, because the child can now tell right from wrong, the child can sin. In the Catholic Church, children traditionally do their first confession of sins at age seven. Mythic consciousness arises when the mind—or ego—of the child develops to the point where it becomes the lord and master of the child's inner world. The mind or ego becomes the monotheistic god of the psyche and all other inner realities—fantasies, dreams, emotions, impulses[2]—are brought under mental control. This ego, which is archetypally male, is now projected into the sky and becomes the monotheistic, patriarchal Sky God.

The mythic level is a conformist, law-and-order level. Children learn to define themselves by concrete and definite rules and roles (boys play ball, girls play with dolls) and see their self-worth in following these "laws." This level is also ethnocentric or sociocentric; that is, everything in the child's parochial world is seen as the "true" and the "best." If Daddy and Mommy belong to a certain religious denomination, race, color, ethnic group, income level, or political party, these become the "correct" and "true" ones, often the *only* true ones, all others being inferior or false. One's nation or ethnic group or religion is typically seen as the greatest in the world, blessed by God beyond all others.

At the mythic level, children no longer believe that they order the world around them by uttering a magic word. *But they believe that God can do so.* If it would take a miracle of supernatural intervention to turn broccoli into ice cream or, more seriously, to save their mother from breast cancer or safeguard their older brother fighting in a foxhole in Afghanistan, children have no doubt that God can do it. For the child believes, according to the level of egoism proper to the mythic level, that God exists primarily to fulfill the child's needs.

Children use their emerging reason to reinterpret the previous magical world. Religious myths and symbols, therefore, are now understood in a concrete, literal, rational way. The three wise men, for example, did literally follow a star to Bethlehem, and Mary gave birth to Jesus, not as other mothers do, but in some sort of miraculous fashion. God made the world in six calendar days, and Moses raised a rod and parted the Red Sea.

At the mythic level of consciousness, children are "good" if they follow the rules of the parents (God for the child) and "bad" if they break them. Children learn to see their intrinsic self-worth in terms of external rules and roles, which therefore are taken with deadly seriousness. Children assume that everything in their immediate cultural environment is the only true way to do things and the only true way to think. They cannot think otherwise at this stage.

The mythic level, despite the emergence of the child's mind and the shifting of the child's self-centeredness from the individual to the immediate culture, is still a very egocentric level. Tolerance and understanding for other points of view and behaviors, and compassion for people who hold these views and practice these behaviors, are simply not possible for a child or adult with mythic consciousness. Nor can they see any good reason for even attempting such tolerance because, for them, this would be a betrayal of their external God, the God whose rules and roles define their entire self-worth.

Because the child's very worth as a person is seen in terms of these rules and roles, the child aggressively defends them. Other children who follow different rules, have different behaviors, or are otherwise "different" must be mocked and strenuously opposed because they threaten the child's sense of self.

For the adult Christian whose consciousness has not progressed beyond the mythic level of consciousness, it is important to convert the whole world to the one true Christian religion (and to make sure that governments enact laws that agree with what the believer has been taught are "Christian" morals) because in the end this is the only real way the mythic believer can safely secure her own righteousness. This requires the elimination, by conversion or otherwise, of all "others" because all such "others" are seen as threatening the mythic believer's externally defined sense of worth. A mythic Christian cannot rest until the whole world thinks and does as she has been schooled as a child to think and do.

The Christian adult who is stuck in mythic consciousness will see the followers of other religions (or "isms" such as Marxism or feminism) as "evil" and probably headed for hell. It is perfectly all right for the mythic believer to try to commandeer the police powers of the state (as was done in the Middle Ages) to impose her belief system on others. After all, it is for the others' own good that they submit to the "truth" as the mythic believer assumes the truth to be. It may even be all right at times to kill people of other religions (or even other denominations of Christianity) to "save their souls."

People at the mythic level are psychologically incapable of thinking "globally." They usually neither think about, nor care about, such matters as the global environment, health, financial condition, or population. They are normally totally centered upon their own financial, familial, ethnic, sectarian, and nationalistic concerns (e.g., they vote based primarily on "what's in it for me or my group"). Anything universal (e.g., the United Nations) does not concern them. If they do happen to think about the United Nations, they are very likely to see it primarily in terms of a threat to themselves, their values, and their group.

At the cultural level, monotheistic mythic consciousness was a great step forward from the world of tribes because people did not need to meet the materialistic requirement of blood kinship to belong. In theory, monotheism was universal because anyone could belong *provided* they converted and accepted as literal and God-ordained the myths, authority figures (uniformly patriarchal), and rules and roles (often quite materialistic, e.g., you may not eat pork) of the religion. Mythic consciousness allowed tribes to unite to form the ancient empires and, much later, today's nation states. Monotheism, however universal (or catholic with a small "c") it was in theory, was not (and never has been) universal in practice.

The "God of Abraham, Isaac, and Jacob" was most assuredly not the God of the Canaanites, Philistines, or Midianites. As for the last, God ordered Moses, after Moses had killed all the Midianite men, burnt their homes, and taken their livestock, to kill all the male children and the nonvirginal women, leaving only the virgins to be taken away to service Moses' troops (Num. 31:15–18). The monotheistic God was ethnocentric, not universal, for the simple reason that the emerging concrete, operational mind (what psychologists call the mythic consciousness of today's seven- to 14-year-olds) is not capable of abstract universal thinking. God did not love everybody. God only cared about those who followed the particular rules and roles of the particular culture and religion, in this case, the Hebrews.

For the same reason, mythic-level Christianity and Islam, as the scions of Judaism, have never been universal except in theory. The only way they could become universal, given the constraints of mythic consciousness, would be to convert the rest of the world—something both have attempted (and failed) to do. Nor will they ever succeed, for their materialistic approach to universalism misses the spiritual point.

The Old Testament describes in great detail the emergence in human history of monotheistic mythic consciousness in place of the magical consciousness that previously prevailed. The Hebrews were the first Western monotheistic culture. The Bible (Gen. 17:4–5) tells of Abraham, who became the unifying patriarchal Father of many nations (tribes) and was a devotee of the one unifying God who replaced the many tribal gods. This one God was understood primarily as a Sky God who lived in the heavens and was separate and apart from humans. Abraham, the Bible says, intended to sacrifice Isaac, his only begotten son, to appease this one God, but an angel appeared and told him that human sacrifice, a staple in tribal days, was no longer necessary (Gen. 22:1–18). Sacrifice continued, but only of animals.

I believe that sacrificing animals represented the sacrificing (putting under the control of the mind or ego) of the lower animal-like parts of human consciousness, particularly aggression and sexuality, so that the tribes could live together in a more or less civilized fashion.

For the same reason, because they were seen as representing the body, emotions, sexuality, and "baser" human nature in general, women were demoted to second-class status, and a host of sexual and gender role restrictions were imposed upon both men and women. This was felt to be crucially necessary. Why? Because, the essence of the shift from magical to mythic consciousness is the struggle of the mind (seen as "male") to take control of the human psyche. So it was imperative that the mind (and therefore men, especially given the male's aggressive and sexually promiscuous instincts) not be tempted to regress to the old level. Women, representing the body, sexuality, and emotions like aggression, had to be kept under wraps. From today's rational point of view, of course, this was very confused thinking. But it's the type of confused thinking endemic to the concrete operational or mythic level. Biological gender, a physical (materialistic) affair, was confused with spiritual archetypes that saw mind as "masculine" and emotions and sexuality as "feminine."

Homosexual men (no one has ever been much bothered by homosexual women)—that is, men who were inclined to take the sexual role of women—were suppressed altogether. They were seen as more dangerous than women to the new mind-set, for they were males who, in a sense, subverted the whole new patriarchal worldview. Not only Judaism, but also Christianity and Islam, the descendants of Judaism, have kept women (and gay men) under wraps ever since.

Westerners tend to be horrified by the head-to-toe *burqas* that women in Saudi Arabia are required to wear and by the Taliban's summary execution of gay men. But one should remember that only two generations ago the Arabians were a tribal culture of nomadic Bedouin. So too, though less nomadic, were the Afghans. Westerners need to be realistic when it comes to Islam. It has taken Christianity five hundred years to move from the mythic to the rational worldview. We cannot expect Islam, isolated during most of that period, to make the transition overnight.

Moses, a later patriarch, introduced God's Ten Commandments,[3] and his immediate successors created hundreds of concrete commandments and laws, rules and roles, which the mythic believer had to follow to be sure he was doing right by God. The books of Leviticus and Deuteronomy, chock-full of roles and rules, came from this mythic thinking. No longer was the tribe the sole mediator between the person and God. The individual, now that the inner individual ego had begun to operate, was expected to actually do something himself to secure his worth in God's eyes.

At both the individual and societal levels, human self-consciousness (the "I") was no longer identified with biology and emotions but began to be identified with the mind, the male Sky God being the projection of this mind and the patriarch being the Sky God's spokesperson on Earth. God's relationship with humans was seen as a legal contract or covenant.

If you obeyed the rules, God would be pleased. If not, God would be displeased. Since this God was a projection of the human ego (made in man's image and likeness), he could be jealous, angry, vengeful, arbitrary, and judgmental, as well as kind and supportive.

The mythic level of religion and culture has been the dominant level of human consciousness all over the world since around the time of Abraham (or at least the time of Moses). It still predominates in Islam. It is still powerful among Jewish sects in Israel. And it dominated Christianity until Galileo and the rise of modern abstract science.

When a modern American or Western European child reaches adolescence, he is expected by the current Western culture to leave the mythic level behind and to embrace the scientific, abstract, higher-level thinking that, since the Enlightenment of the eighteenth century, we have called reason, and which the psychologists now call formal operational thinking. When the American Declaration of Independence of July 4, 1776, proclaimed that "All men are created equal . . . endowed by their Creator with certain inalienable Rights," that was not the operation of mythic-level thinking.

Despite the treatment of slaves and the omission of women, it was an attempt, on the philosophical, political, and theological levels, to assert the principle of true human universality. It meant *all* humans are created equal, not just those of a particular religion or ethnic group or those who adhered to this or that cultural or moral set of rules and roles. The "Creator" referred to by the Declaration is a true universal Creator, the maker of the entire universe and the originator of all the universal scientific laws by which the universe operates.[4]

The Declaration was a major turning point in human history. It was as significant for the rise of human consciousness as the Ten Commandments were to the prior leap of consciousness.[5] We are still elaborating, now worldwide, on the implications of this leap to the fourth level of human consciousness, the *rational*.

The Declaration, and later the American Constitution with its Bill of Rights, was momentous in another respect. Unlike in medieval times when power flowed *downward* from God to the Pope and/or the King, then down to the nobility, and finally to the people, the Declaration and the Constitution envisioned power flowing *upward* from the people to the rulers, the rulers having only those powers delegated to them by the people. Thus was established the basic principle of liberal democracy.

Fundamentalists, of course, resist a universal God such as the God described in the Declaration of Independence. When Rev. Pat Robertson realized that President George W. Bush intended to fund the charitable works of non-Christian religions, he suddenly lost his early enthusiasm for Bush's faith-based initiative. A recent president of the Southern Baptist Convention rejected a universal God by saying that Allah and the Christian God are different. A recent stunning example of this type of thinking were the remarks of Lieutenant General William G. Boykin, President Bush's undersecretary of defense for intelligence. Referring to a Muslim leader he fought in 1993 in Somalia, General Boykin remarked, "I knew that my God was bigger than his."[6]

President Bush has gotten into hot water on this issue. On a state visit to the United Kingdom, in response to a reporter's question, the president stated that he believes Christians and Muslims worship the same God. Immediately, Richard Land of the Southern Baptist Convention said that Bush "is simply mistaken," and Rev. Ted Haggard, president of the National Association of Evangelicals, issued a statement saying that "The Christian God encourages freedom, love, forgiveness, prosperity, and health. The Muslim god appears to value the opposite." Land reminded people that Bush was no theologian.[7]

But isn't there only one God? Yes, of course. Perhaps the greatest and most fundamental truth of all three great monotheistic religions—Judaism, Christianity, and Islam—is that there is only one God, the creator of heaven and Earth and of all beings. But believers at the mythic level simply cannot grasp this most fundamental teaching because they are unable to think universally. They are so ethnocentric (my group is better than your group, my nation is better than your nation, my God is better than your God) that they distort even this most basic teaching of monotheism.

They have not yet made the conceptual leap from one God to true universality. When they talk of one God they mean *their* God. At the mythic level the child (or adult) thinks *concretely,* which is why mythic thinking is called concrete operational thinking. For example, during the Gulf War, a young boy of about eight asked me why we were fighting Iraq. I was trying to formulate an answer he would understand when something else he said made me realize he meant "a rock," not "Iraq." He had tried to understand the TV news in a way he could grasp, but he could only understand something concrete like a rock, not an abstract concept like the nation of Iraq. This is concrete operational thinking.

Similarly, the fundamentalist believes there is only one God, but he sees that different religions not only have different names for God (e.g., Allah, Brahma), but have different *concrete* roles, rules, customs, rituals, dogmas (Buddhists seek salvation from suffering rather than sin), and even moral strictures (Islam prohibits alcohol but endorses polygamy). Then, because his God is fully enmeshed in the particular ethnocentric or sociocentric concrete roles, rules, and customs of his religion, he cannot see that his God and the others are the same. He cannot grasp that the one God can have varied revelations, scriptures, and commandments as God is understood, interpreted, and sought by people of different times and cultures.

He also has not yet grown in compassion enough to realize that all these other human beings can be as fully and sincerely devoted to God as he is, often more so. You have to be able to think at the abstract rational level, that of "formal operational thinking," in order to grasp these concepts, and you have to have a universal compassion to appreciate the sincere paths of non-Christian seekers and the seekers of other Christian denominations.

I am critical of fundamentalism regarding the points I make in this book about the limitations of mythic level consciousness. But I recognize the value and truth of mythic consciousness and its legitimate place as a level of human awareness. I often watch fundamentalists preach on TV and am impressed by the sincerity of many and by their love for God. Whenever someone, say a young man who has been a gang member (a modern form of tribalism) and drug pusher, ruled by impulse and emotion, comes forward to be born again and accept Jesus as his personal savior, I am always deeply moved. Spiritually, the young man has graduated *upward* into fundamentalism.

Since the Declaration of Independence, rational level consciousness has increasingly dominated America, and now, at the beginning of the twenty-first century, it is coming to dominate the entire world. The mythic Sky God has no place in this new worldview, except among children aged seven to 14. Part 1 of this book examines why belief in a mythic Sky God has died for millions in the Christian world.

1
How God Died–A History

The question of the death of God has been with us for at least the past 120 years. In 1882, the German philosopher Friedrich Nietzsche (1844–1900) wrote about a fictional character, a madman, who runs into a marketplace shouting, "God is dead." Nietzsche has the madman later that same day enter various churches where, in each, he chants a requiem for God. When asked what he is doing, the madman answers, "What are these churches now, if they are not the tombs and monuments of God?"[1] Even though Nietzsche, then probably Europe's most brilliant and renowned philosopher, was careful to place these words in the mouth of a fictional madman, this passage caused a furor, one that has not subsided to this day. Nietzsche had struck a nerve.

In the second edition of the same book, in 1887, Nietzsche

explained that by "God is dead" his fictional character meant that "belief in the Christian God has become unbelievable."[2] And indeed this was true, not only for Nietzsche, but also for an increasing number of European (and some American) scientifically minded intellectuals as the nineteenth century drew to a close.

Disillusionment with the Christian God had been growing since Galileo (1564–1642). Using the telescope that Hans Lippershey (1570–1619) had invented, Galileo confirmed the theory of the Polish priest Nicolaus Copernicus (1473–1543) that the Earth was not the center of the universe. Prior to Galileo, Christians had believed the cosmology set forth in the Bible (and assumed by the Christian Creed), namely, that the sun and planets moved around the Earth, that the stars were "fixed" in a heavenly vault or ceiling, that heaven was on the other side of the vault, and that hell, the underworld, was under the (flat) Earth. Science appeared to support this cosmology: The most authoritative astronomer until Galileo, the ancient Egyptian Claudius Ptolemy (85–165), had devised a cosmology that was centered on the Earth.

Most Christians also believed that God lived in heaven with his only begotten Son, Jesus Christ; that this Son had "come down" from heaven to Earth by being born of a virgin by the Holy Spirit;[3] that Jesus had later returned to heaven in his resurrected, i.e., resuscitated, body; and that Jesus would someday return bodily from heaven, riding on the clouds. Galileo and his successors' more accurate description of the physical universe destroyed the cosmology underlying these doctrinal formulations of belief.

Three centuries before Galileo, the great theologian Thomas Aquinas had stated that because truth is one, there could be no contradiction between the truths of faith and the truths of reason. But Galileo's discovery seemed to the churchmen of his time to threaten that unity. Rather than reexamine their dogmas and their interpretations of scripture, however, the response of the Church was to force Galileo to retract his views and to place him under house arrest for the remainder of his life. Robert Bellarmine (1542–1621), the Jesuit Cardinal who prosecuted Galileo, declaimed, "To assert that the earth revolves around the sun is as erroneous as to claim that Jesus was not born of a virgin."[4]

It was only in 1992 that the Church, through Pope John Paul II, like Copernicus a Polish priest and a graduate of the University of Krakow, admitted that the Church had been wrong in forbidding Galileo to teach Copernican cosmology. (The Church lifted the ban on the teaching of Copernican cosmology in 1820.)

Although it is the Catholic Church that has taken the heat over the years for condemning Galileo, it was actually the Protestant reformers with their literal interpretation of scripture who first condemned the sun-centered theory. Before Copernicus's book was even published, Martin Luther condemned him as an "upstart astrologer" who dared to contradict scripture. John Calvin asked, "Who will dare to place the authority of Copernicus above that of the Holy Spirit?" Luther, Calvin, and Melanchthon thought Copernicus's ideas a heresy that needed to be suppressed. These condemnations were issued many years before the Catholic Church moved against Galileo. One of the reasons it finally did move against him was so as not to be criticized by the reformers for laxness in safeguarding the scriptures.[5]

The Galileo controversy began a long-standing battle between the Church and science, which in many respects is still under way. For example, in 1973 the psychiatric profession, after almost a century of study and the treatment of tens of thousands of patients by thousands of psychiatrists, officially declared that from a scientific and medical point of view homosexuality is not a mental disorder but a normal variant of human sexuality. Most of the Christian Church, including the Vatican, still insists otherwise, based on a dubious understanding of three or four isolated passages of scripture.

After Galileo, Isaac Newton (1642–1727) and countless other scientists discovered more of the physical, chemical, and biological laws and processes that govern the universe. These discoveries gave "God" less and less to do. It got so that the Deists (who counted among their number several of the Founding Fathers of the United States), although they believed there was a God, thought that God, having once created the universe and its laws, was thereafter a sort of absentee landlord who no longer intervened on Earth or anywhere else in the physical universe. It was only one further step to dispense with God altogether.

Adam Smith (1723–1790) and Karl Marx (1818–1883) showed that even the economy operated according to laws that could be discovered and applied. Marx, a brilliant philosopher and economist, was also an atheist who wrote that "religion was the opiate of the people" because, as traditionally taught, religion focused people on the next world, not on changing the economic injustice and oppressions of this world. Marx and Friedrich Engels, in 1848, wrote the *Communist Manifesto,* the principles of a new materialistic Communist party that would seek to disestablish unbridled capitalist economic injustice through political action.

In 1859, Charles Darwin (1809–1882) startled everyone by providing evidence that animal species, including presumably humans, evolved on Earth over countless eons by a process of natural selection. Darwin's discovery rocked the Christian world and was strongly opposed by such as Samuel Wilberforce (1805–1873), the Church of England's bishop of Oxford. Up until then most Christians, who took Genesis literally, had believed in a God who, after creating the universe and all the animals in six calendar days,[6] had with his own hands made Adam, the first man, out of mud, and then made Eve, the first woman, out of a rib taken from Adam's side. This God, who was a separate being (a male separate being), had actually walked about in the Garden of Eden and spoken with Adam and Eve after he had breathed life into them. But after 1859, if evolution were accepted as true, the Garden of Eden story had to be seen as myth, not history.

The theological implications of evolution were staggering. No historical Garden of Eden meant that Adam and Eve did not *fall* from Paradise. Rather, the theory of evolution soon asserted, humans had *ascended* from the first one-celled animals by way of multicelled animals, fish, amphibians, mammals, and primates. If there was no historical fall, no "original sin," then there was no need for a redemption from a fall that didn't happen, and no need for the Ptolemaic God in the sky to send his son to Earth to redeem us by being crucified.

There was also, then, no transmission of the "original sin" of Adam and Eve to all their human descendants (by way of the injection of the male seed during the sexual intercourse that resulted in conception, according to Saint Augustine's bizarrely materialistic theory). For a great many educated Christians, Darwin's discovery, coupled with that of Copernicus, made God, as Nietzsche's madman said, "become unbelievable."[7]

Science, however, was not the only force undermining Christianity and its God. Christians were often their own worst enemies. Two years after Darwin published *On the Origin of Species,* civil war broke out in the United States over the issue of slavery, the single most important moral issue of the nineteenth century. Although many Christians were active in the abolitionist movement, large segments of the American Protestant Church—southern Presbyterians as well as southern Baptists and Methodists—had broken away from their denominations rather than oppose slavery.[8]

Generally, these southern Christians cited the Bible as justification for slavery. They saw Africans as descendents of Ham, whose son Canaan was cursed into slavery by Noah (Gen. 9:25). Thundered Senator James Henry Hammond of South Carolina, "The doom of Ham has been branded on the form and features of his African descendants. The hand of fate has united his color and destiny. Man cannot separate what God hath joined."[9] Under this scriptural interpretation, God had ordained slavery and it was not for man to abolish that institution.

Jefferson Davis, the president of the Confederate States, argued, "[Slavery] was established by decree of Almighty God and is sanctioned in the Bible in both Testaments from Genesis to Revelations."[10] As for Catholics, not a single American bishop formally condemned slavery during the Civil War, and the bishop of Natchitoches, Louisiana, actually published a pastoral letter in support of slavery, using the same reference to the biblical Canaan.

Southern Christians actually had a point. Nowhere in the Bible is slavery condemned by God. Instead, the God of the Bible accepts slavery as moral and normal. In Leviticus 25:44, God authorizes the Jews to make slaves of the heathen tribes around them. In Proverbs 29:19, God recommends that slaves be physically punished rather than merely reprimanded. In Exodus 21:20, God does prescribe punishment for killing a slave, "but if the slave survives for a day or two, he [the master] shall not be punished: for the slave is his property." In Exodus 21:7-10, God authorizes Jewish men to sell their daughters into slavery. Deuteronomy 20:13-14 instructs the Jews that, after God has delivered an enemy town to them, they are to kill all the men and make slaves of the women and children.

Even the New Testament is no help on the moral issue. For example, both Saint Peter and Saint Paul instruct slaves to obey their masters (1 Pet. 2:18; Eph. 6:5). In 1866, one year after the American Civil War, Pope Pius IX summarized Christian teaching as follows:

> Slavery itself, considered as such in its essential nature, is not at all contrary to the natural and divine law . . . It is not contrary to the natural and divine law for a slave to be sold, bought, exchanged or given.[11]

In short, neither the Church nor the Judeo-Christian God was of much if any help in resolving the greatest moral question of the nineteenth century. It can even be said that the slaves were freed not because of Christianity, its Bible, and its God, but in spite of them.

In 1832, Pope Gregory XVI had condemned freedom of the press and freedom of opinion or conscience because these tended to jeopardize the authority of European monarchs (including him). He also defended book-burning (citing Acts 19:19, which describes some magicians burning their books). In December 1864, just as the American Civil War was coming to an end, Pius IX, speaking, he believed, as God's representative on Earth (Matt. 16:18–19), issued his famous (or infamous) *Syllabus of Errors,* one of the most astonishing documents of the modern era.

The *Syllabus* was a list of 80 modern "errors," each of which Pius condemned. It is an error, he wrote, that "Divine revelation [the Bible] is . . . subject to a continual and indefinite progress, corresponding with the advancement of human reason" (#5). It is an error, he said, to think that "In the books of the Old and the New Testament there are contained mythical inventions" (#7). It is also an error to think that "The decrees of the Apostolic See and of the Roman congregations impede the true progress of science" (#12). He said that it is wrong to think that "Every man is free to embrace and profess that religion which, guided by the light of reason, he shall consider true" (#15). He held that "The Catholic Church is the only true religion" (#21), that the Church may use force to impose its beliefs on non-Catholics (#24), and that neither Protestantism nor any non-Christian religion could bring a soul to salvation (#16–#18).

Pius said it was wrong that public schools be "freed from all ecclesiastical authority, control and interference" (#47). He said it was error to think that "The Church ought to be separated from the State, and the State from the Church" (#55). It was error, he said, that divorce could "be decreed by civil authority" (#67) or that the form of marriage could be established by civil authority (#71). It is error to think, he wrote, that "In the present day it is no longer expedient that the Catholic religion should be held as the only religion of the State, to the exclusion of all other forms of worship" (#77). It was wrong, he said, for Catholic countries to allow non-Catholics "the public exercise of their own peculiar worship" (#78). And finally, it was wrong to believe that "The Roman Pontiff can, and ought to, reconcile himself, and come to terms with progress [evolution], liberalism [i.e., liberal democracy], and modern civilization" (#80).[12]

The *Syllabus* raised a firestorm of criticism among intellectuals all over Europe and in North America. It probably did more to discredit Catholicism (and the Pope as God's "spokesperson" on Earth) than any other single document issued in modern times. It was an angry, reactionary document, responding negatively to all the major intellectual, social, and political advances of the day.[13]

Pius opposed liberal democracy. He opposed secular public schools. He opposed religious tolerance and the separation of Church and State. He opposed scientific advances that threatened traditional understandings of scripture. He was angry that the Church was losing its exclusive authority over marriage and education and that the Church, in many Christian countries, could no longer commandeer the police powers of the State to punish nonbelievers and disobedient Catholics. And he was especially angry that democratic forces had already (in 1861) taken most of the Papal States, that considerable part of Italy over which he had been the autocratic, monarchical temporal ruler, and were threatening the rest of his kingdom, including Rome.[14]

In 1868, by the decree *Non Expedit,* Pius forbade Italian Catholics from voting in or taking part in Italian elections, a decree that lasted until well into the twentieth century. Finally, in 1869, he called a Vatican Council for the sole purpose of having himself declared infallible, a decree which he practically bludgeoned the bishops into adopting and one that has ever since greatly complicated relations between Catholicism and the Protestant, Orthodox, and Anglican branches of the Church.[15] Secular intellectuals saw the decree as an arrogant power grab, as if one person, no matter his office, could fix any truth in propositional cement for all time. The decree on infallibility was issued just days before the army of the Italian republic liberated Rome.[16]

As if these self-inflicted wounds were not enough for the Church, there were still more as the nineteenth century came to an end. In a prelude to the Nazi Holocaust, Christians in Russia and Poland committed pogrom after pogrom against their Jewish neighbors, burning whole villages and killing thousands, their actions often condoned by Catholic and Orthodox church officials. In Rome, Pius IX called Jews "dogs," and the official Vatican newspaper ran viciously anti-Semitic articles, even accusing Jews of using the blood of Christian children in ritual sacrifice. In virtually all of Latin America, in an exercise of overt racism, Native Americans, blacks, and mestizos (mixed-bloods) could not be ordained as priests. Only pure-blood Spanish need apply.

Before 1900, still another front opened. Another intellectual giant, Sigmund Freud (1856–1939), published nine works on psychoanalysis, a revolutionary approach to human psychology. He published 21 more papers by the time of the First World War. Freud established that there were scientific laws underlying the operation of the human psyche. He discovered that much of what had been called "demons" or "the Devil" in the past were really mental or emotional illnesses, psychoneuroses, and psychoses.

Under the new psychology, the Ptolemaic Sky God (who could be angry, jealous, vengeful, and judgmental as well as loving and merciful) was shown to be a psychological projection into outer space of the rational male egos of the persons doing the projecting. The Sky God was a mental construct created by humans, a view that turned creation upside down (it seemed that human beings created God, not vice versa). Finally, the work of Freud and his successors showed the immense psychological and spiritual damage that had been done to Christians by the repressive sexual teachings of the Christian Church.

In the meantime, especially during the second half of the nineteenth century, Protestant biblical scholars in Germany and England, followed by a few Catholics, armed with a new appreciation of history and new approaches to the critical examination of texts, began questioning much of the Bible. They wanted to discover such things as who wrote its various books, when they were written, where, and in what form (poetry, narrative, history, legend, myth).

One of the first things they realized, by a careful examination of the texts, was that Moses was not the author of the first five books of the Bible, called the Pentateuch or Torah, as both Jews and Christians had believed for centuries. One big hint: Exodus, the second book, describes the death of Moses. How could Moses, now deceased, describe his own death and then keep writing? And how was it possible for one man to have so many different styles of writing, such shifting vocabularies, to refer to so many different historical time periods? Obviously, it wasn't possible.

The scholars determined that the four accounts of Jesus' Resurrection in Matthew, Mark, Luke, and John were so radically different that they could not be reconciled. For example, Matthew 28:1 has two women come to the tomb (Mary Magdalene and another Mary). John 20:1 has only Mary Magdalene. Luke 20:10 has three women (Mary Magdalene, Joanna, and Mary, the mother of James). Mark 16:1 also has three but substitutes Salome for Joanna. In John 20:1, it was still dark; in Mark 16:2, the sun had risen. Matthew has an angel sitting on the rolled-away stone (Matt. 28:2). Mark 16:5 has a "young man" sitting at the right. Luke 24:4 has two men standing, not sitting. John 20:1 has no one except Mary Magdalene. Did Peter go to the tomb by himself (Luke 24:12) or was it Peter and John (John 20:2–8)? Did the disciples believe (Matt. 28:16) or disbelieve the women (Mark 16:11; Luke 24:11)?

There are also contradictions in the gospels about whom Jesus appeared to first, with 1 Corinthians 15:5 adding to that particular confusion. Either the authors of the Gospels were not telling the truth, or they were telling a story with a theological rather than a historical meaning.[17] The same, the new biblical science showed, applied to dozens of other passages of scripture.

Although Protestant scholars in Europe and North America operated with a large degree of freedom (though not without intense opposition), Pope Leo XIII (1878–1903) and later Pope Pius X (1903–1914) tried to rein in and control the new approaches to scripture by Catholics. Pius X issued his own syllabus called *Lamentabili Sane* in 1907, in which 65 propositions were condemned, 38 of them relating to biblical criticism. He even went so far as to require every priest and seminary professor to take an oath against what he called "Modernism." The oath, which drove many more European priests and intellectuals away from the Church, required them, among other things, to "reject that method of judging and interpreting Sacred Scripture which . . . embraces the misrepresentations of the rationalists" and prohibited them from interpreting the scriptures "with the same liberty of judgement that is common in the investigation of all ordinary historical documents."[18]

Many mythic-level Protestants were also alarmed by Darwinism and biblical criticism. Between 1909 and 1915, some conservative American Protestant scholars published a series of pamphlets entitled *The Fundamentals: A Testimony to Truth,* from which we get the term "fundamentalist," and which marked the beginning of the fundamentalist movement in the United States. They insisted on the inerrancy of every word of the Bible, Jesus' biological virgin birth, the physical resurrection (resuscitation) of Jesus, the "substitutionary" theory of atonement (i.e., that Jesus died to appease his Father for the world's sins), and a literal, physical "second coming" of Jesus of Nazareth to judge the world. All these, of course, were under attack by the new sciences.

At the turn of the century, Albert Einstein (1879–1955) revolutionized physics by showing that time and space existed relative to each other. Both were products of and essential to the structure of the physical universe. Time apart from space made no sense. What then about eternity, which most Christians believed was an *infinite duration of time* after death during which they would be rewarded in heaven or punished in hell? If time made no sense except in the context of the physical universe, what credence could be given to the belief in "infinite" time?[19]

August 1914 brought the death of Pius X, the start of World War I, and the end of the centuries-long era of Christian Europe. The war unleashed forces that would forever change the face and thought of that continent, long the stronghold of Christianity. As the war began, Protestant prelates called upon God to bless the troops of the Kaiser's German Empire as they headed into battle. Orthodox prelates called upon God to bless the troops of the Czar's Russian Empire. Catholic prelates called upon God to bless the troops of the Holy Roman Empire of Austria-Hungary.

There is no evidence that God heard any of their prayers. All three Christian empires were destroyed in the so-called war to end all wars. The remaining two Christian empires, the British and the French, would be destroyed by the bigger war yet to come. By the time World War I ended, atheistic Communism had triumphed in Russia and belief in God was dead among hundreds of thousands of European and American intellectuals.

For the past three thousand years, the Judeo-Christian tradition (and most believers of other faiths) has held what the psychologists and theorists of the evolution of human consciousness now call a mythic conception of God. In other words, God has been seen as a being who lives in the sky (heaven), a being separate from humans and all Creation, and as a being who in response to prayer (or to punish) supernaturally intervenes, whether often or from time to time, in the human condition.

In Christianity, this mythic conception of God has almost completely colored our understanding of Jesus and his teachings. Jesus has been primarily understood not as a human being who realized his own divinity, but as a god or divine being who was sent down from the sky. This god then died on the cross to appease his Father, the Sky God, for the sins of humanity (supposedly incurred long ago by the first humans, Adam and Eve, in the Garden of Eden). This has been the central myth of Christianity. Until recent years, literal belief in this myth has been virtually a "given" among believers in all Christian countries.

For millions today, however, the central myth of Christianity no longer holds true. For millions of Christians (and Jews for that matter), the mythic Sky God is now dead. Evolution has destroyed belief in Eden, the Garden of Paradise in which man was supposedly created. Astronomy has destroyed belief in a physical heaven, located above the vault of the stars, to which resurrected bodies will someday go, and to which Jesus bodily ascended.

History, archeology, and other sciences have failed to reveal any supernatural interventions by a divine being in human affairs. Even when millions of human beings cried out in agony during the two world wars and the Holocaust that accompanied the second, intervention by the Sky God was nowhere to be found. Physics, mathematics, chemistry, biology, and other sciences have demonstrated that the world is ruled by laws that man can learn to manipulate. We can send people to the moon, genetically engineer new crops, clone mammals, and do thousands of other things without the slightest recourse to anything or anyone supernatural.

Biology, psychology, and biblical criticism, among other sciences, have made us more appreciative of Jesus' humanness, a humanness that the Church has always affirmed but seldom emphasized. Jesus of Nazareth is more and more appreciated as a man of his times, his history, and a product of his Jewish tradition. As for the God whom Jesus called "Father," the whole idea of God as a vengeful father who needed appeasement by means of the blood of his son has become more and more grotesque to the modern sensibility.

While this decline in belief has been occurring, the Church has been of little help. The Church, both Catholic and Protestant, has taken primarily a defensive and authoritarian posture. From Galileo's sun-centered solar system to Darwin's discovery of evolution to modern psychology's discovery of the naturalness of homosexuality, the Church has militantly opposed one scientific breakthrough after another. It has also largely failed to provide enlightened moral leadership on profound moral issues from slavery to women's and gay rights to the supreme horror of the Holocaust. The Church's role as a credible spokesperson for the mythic Sky God has fallen along with the Sky God himself.

2
Acceptance of the Death of God

Dr. Elisabeth Kübler-Ross, in her landmark book *On Death and Dying*, describes the five stages that dying persons normally go through. They are, in order, denial, anger, bargaining, depression (mourning), and acceptance. Culturally, the death of God has also gone through these five stages. The Church's treatment of Galileo was classic denial. Galileo was forbidden to teach and his writings were placed on the "Index of Forbidden Books," which Christians were prohibited from reading. In other words, unpleasant truth was to be swept under a rug and not mentioned or written of anymore. It was to be denied.

The reaction of Pius IX to the new sciences and the cultural worldview they brought with them was classic second-stage anger. Pius IX was a very angry man. He hurled condemnations at any idea or any person with whom he disagreed. By Pius's time, the new intellectual worldview, which included the death of the mythic Sky God, had gotten too powerful to be swept under a rug. Anger was his response.

Bargaining, the third stage, is an attempt to accept the new while still holding onto the old. Pius XII's acceptance of biblical criticism in 1943, John Paul II's grudging acceptance of evolution in 1996, and even the decrees of the Second Vatican Council are examples of bargaining.[1] The new truths are accepted but the old worldview is not given up. There has been no change in the ancient Christian Creed even though it is written entirely in mythological language that is incomprehensible to the contemporary person who does not accept myths as literally true. Thus the myths of Fall, Redemption, Resurrection, and Ascension are still preached in most Christian churches as if they were literally true. The same old hymns about how Jesus came down from heaven and atoned to his father for our sins by dying on the cross are still sung every Sunday in countless Christian churches.

Christians go to church on Sunday as if entering a time warp, putting the modern rational worldview aside for an hour or two to submit to the old mythic worldview. Then they reemerge into the rational worldview by which they operate their lives and professions during the week.

That is, if they still go to church, for many do not because they are tired of this weekly regression and the irrelevance of the mythic worldview to their lives. Many of those who continue to go to church have entered the fourth stage of dying—depression and mourning. They miss the way things were and are bereft. But they see no way back.

Others have gone all the way—into the final stage of acceptance. They have finally accepted the new situation and no longer go to church. They have accepted the rational worldview and the death of God. For them the dying process is complete and they are lost to a Church that still clings to the old.

Although I know of no scientific studies that have interviewed Christians in depth on their reasons for no longer attending church, it seems clear to me from anecdotal evidence, from my own experience with thousands of Christians, and from the lack of church attendance, that many have now accepted the death of the mythic God. They no longer believe in a God who is a separate being, who lives in the sky, and who intervenes in history in response to prayer. This is reflected in, and I believe can be inferred from, the huge increase in the last decade in the number of unchurched Americans. In 1999, Barna Research Group reported that these now number about 65 million, including 40 percent of adults in the west and northeast sections of the United States.

At the beginning of the twenty-first century, what is the state of Christianity and its God? Let us start our examination by returning to Nietzsche's madman.

After the madman had mourned in the churches over the death of God, he returned to the marketplace and fell silent. His listeners fell silent as well. Then he said, "I have come too early, my time is not yet. This tremendous event [the death of God] is still on its way, still wandering; it has not yet reached the ears of men . . . deeds, though done, still require time to be seen and heard."[2] Nietzsche later explains that by this the madman meant that "The event is far too great, too distant, too remote from the multitude's capacity for comprehension even for the tidings of it to be thought of as having *arrived* as yet."[3] (Emphasis in original.)

In other words, belief in Christianity and its God, though sharply declining among European (and some American) intellectuals before World War I, was still very much alive among the multitude of Christians. It would take a long period of time, predicted Nietzsche, for disbelief in God to grow among the masses of the people.

Where are we today? In April 2000, Britain's *Independent* published an article on the findings of Dr. Peter Brierly, a specialist in church attendance. "Church will be dead in 40 years time," read the headline. Dr. Brierly's surveys showed that in 2000 only 7.5% of England's population attended church on Sunday, a loss of 22% in just the previous ten years. Brierly predicted that the trend would continue and that "all claims that Britain is a Christian nation will have to be given up." In a total population of 60 million, Anglican church attendance was down to 980,000, Catholic to 1,230,000, Methodist to 379,700. Baptist attendance had gone up 2% and that of the evangelical or Pentecostal churches 38%,[4] but these gains were not nearly enough to alter the overall decline.

The Institute for Social Research at the University of Michigan reported in its 1995–1997 World Values Survey that 44% of Americans go to church every Sunday. But another survey by the Institute in 1998 found that, although 40% of Americans *said* they went to church every Sunday, only 20% actually did. Ireland had the highest church attendance, at 84%. But by 1999, after a series of priest pedophilia scandals, Irish church attendance had dropped to 50%, according to a poll by Irish Marketing Surveys. In East Germany, attendance dropped from 20% in 1991 to 9% in 1998. The Institute's 1995–1997 survey showed the following attendance figures for other Christian countries: Finland 4%, Sweden 4%, Russia 2%, Ukraine 10%, Serbia 7%, Denmark and Norway 5%, Czech Republic 14%, West Germany 14%, Belgium 44%, Argentina, Chile, and Spain 25%, Poland 55%, France 21% (based on 1991 data), and Australia 16%.

One minister who works with young people said recently (and his views are typical of youth ministers of every denomination) that he thinks the Millennium generation (those born from 1984 to 1999) will reverse the trend. As evidence, he says that the youth he works with (1) are rebelling against their nonchurchgoing parents and (2) like to have boundaries and limits set for them, including moral boundaries. But he is talking about adolescents, who are always simultaneously rebellious and limit-seeking. If he honestly thinks such attitudes will be carried forward during their college and young adult years, I believe he is living in major denial.

The Barna Group, the religious survey group mentioned previously, has reported a huge rise in the United States of the "unchurched," people who haven't gone to church during the past six months. The unchurched now number more than the largest U.S. religion, Roman Catholicism, which claims 62 million.[5] The Catholic figure, though it may impress politicians seeking votes, is false. It is wildly inflated because it counts anyone ever baptized Catholic.

I know Catholic families who have left the Catholic Church for the Episcopalian or Congregational Church because of the treatment of women or other issues; I have witnessed Catholics being accepted as members by the United Church of Christ; and I have attended a Metropolitan Community Church (a gay Christian church) where 85% of the members are ex-Catholics. I am a member of a metaphysical church with 25% Catholic or ex-Catholic membership, and I know many, many New Age Catholics and ex-Catholics. The Buddhist female abbot of a Tibetan Buddhist monastery near Washington, D.C., was raised a Catholic in Brooklyn. The pastor of a Science of Mind church, whom I know, is a former Catholic priest. So too are the pastor of a "Free Catholic" church and the pastor of a black "unity" church. I am sure this is just a tiny tip of the iceberg, and these are only people who have remained deeply religious, not those who have simply walked away from the Church and are now secular.

In the United States, a 1993 in-depth survey of 4,000 adults showed that 30% were totally secular, 29% barely or nominally religious, 22% modestly religious, and 19% seriously religious.[6] A

Gallup poll after the events of 9-11-2001 showed that church attendance immediately shot up to 47%. One is reminded of the famous adage "There are no atheists in foxholes." This sudden rise in attendance incited the fundamentalist evangelist and one-time presidential candidate, the Reverend Pat Robertson, to exclaim that the attack was "bringing about one of the greatest spiritual revivals in the history of America . . . People are turning to God. The churches are full."[7] But by Thanksgiving, the boom was over and attendance was back down to pre-9-11 levels of about 42% (or 21%, if the 1998 Institute survey is correct).

Right after 9-11, I was at a Catholic mass in a town on the New Jersey shore. There was standing room only in the church that Sunday. People had come to find spiritual solace and some kind of spiritually transcendent meaning to the horrible events they had witnessed on TV. Instead, in that particular church, the preacher used the occasion to go on a tirade against abortion, likening mothers who abort and the doctors who assist them to the terrorists who had devastated New York City and Washington, D.C. Abortion was even worse than what the terrorists had done, he asserted, because the victims of abortion were far more numerous. He called on the congregation to enlist in the American Catholic Church's crusade against abortion. This crusade, though styled "pro-life," is actually an attempt to get the Supreme Court to overrule *Roe v. Wade.*

In *Roe v. Wade* (1973), the Supreme Court ruled that in the matter of abortion, over which there was so much philosophical, political, and moral controversy, the moral decision should be made by the person most intimately concerned—the mother—not by the State. The Church wants to overturn the decision so Congress can then pass legislation to recriminalize abortion. The bottom line of the Church's crusade is jail time for women and doctors who disagree with the Church's moral position. Fundamentalist Christian Protestants have the same result in mind.

This is a goal that would no doubt have succeeded in the Middle Ages when the Church claimed even temporal power over kings and princes, but one which is a dubious and almost certainly hopeless political quest in today's pluralistic America.[8] So it was no surprise to me that the churches were back to their normal half-emptiness by Thanksgiving in 2001. People were probably reminded of why they had stopped attending in the first place.

On July 20, 2002, the *Washington Post* reported that seven Christian denominations, whose memberships have been steadily falling, had commissioned a survey to determine what should be done to reverse the trend. The denominations included the Christian Reformed Church, the Episcopal Church, the Evangelical Lutheran Church in America, Lutheran Church–Missouri Synod, Presbyterian Church (U.S.A.), the Reformed Church in America, and the United Church of Christ, together representing about 15 million American Protestants. The conclusion of the survey was that clergy must be specially trained to be charismatic "church builders."

With all due respect to the survey participants, and in light of the history sketched out previously in this book, that will do little or nothing to stem or reverse the tide. Something much more radical is called for, as Episcopal Bishop John Shelby Spong has recognized in his best-selling 1998 book, *Why Christianity Must Change or Die*. Christianity itself must change, and drastically. That is the bottom line. The survey commissioners are church leaders who remain, to a large extent, in denial.

Let us take just one of the participants in the survey, the Lutheran Church–Missouri Synod, to see how much in denial are the leaders of many Christian churches. The same issue of the *Washington Post* that reported the survey reported that Rev. Wallace Shultze, a vice president of that church, had suspended a New York pastor, Rev. David H. Benke. What had Rev.

Benke done wrong? On September 23, 2001, he had appeared at an interfaith prayer service at Yankee Stadium for the victims of 9-11. The service had been organized by New York Mayor Rudolph Guiliani and national TV talk show host Oprah Winfrey. Besides Christians, there were Muslim, Hindu, Jewish, and Sikh clergy participating. Rev. Benke's sin was that he had prayed with "pagans."

Upon Rev. Benke's suspension, the church was deluged with protests with the result that Rev. Shultze was removed from the premier pulpit of the denomination, the broadcast *Lutheran Hour*. Then, Rev. Benke, wanting to assure the *Post* reporter of his orthodoxy, told the reporter that "he believes the Bible is the literal word of God, the theory of evolution is bunk and the only path to salvation is through Jesus Christ."[9] Does one honestly believe that more dynamic "church builders" are going to save a denomination that refuses to accept the change in worldview that has emerged over the past five hundred years and that now dominates the entire scientific and intellectual world?[10]

The Southern Baptist Convention, the largest of the U.S. Protestant denominations, is equally in denial. In early 2002, the convention cut off a sizable part of the income of the Baptist churches in the Washington, D.C., area. The churches' sin? They were not sufficiently hewing to the fundamentalist line of those who in recent years had taken over the Southern Baptist Convention and were busy installing orthodox dogma (for example, that wives should be subservient to their husbands, as the Bible says) in seminaries and churches, where for the previous several hundred years Baptists had taken pride in their independence and freedom from dogma.

Had the Washington-area churches gotten too independent? No—no more so than Baptist churches have always been. But their sometime liberalism on homosexuality, for example (i.e., their accommodation to the view of scientific psychology), could not be tolerated by the fundamentalists who had taken over the church. After all, did not God himself say, in Leviticus, that men who lie with men should be stoned to death? And did not God, in anger, wipe out the cities of Sodom and Gomorrah because some men there wanted to lie with some angels? The angels were visiting Lot, a nephew of Abraham. Lot protected the angels. It was not explained what angels were doing walking around on Earth in bodies in the first place, and why, if they were angels, they needed Lot to protect them.

The story is obviously mythical and perhaps an attempt by the ancient Hebrews, given their idea of God, to make sense of the destruction of the two cities, probably by an earthquake.[11] Some fundamentalists today, who adhere to the same old vengeful God, think in the same way. For example, after 9-11, Rev. Jerry Falwell said that the World Trade Center had been destroyed because God was punishing America for tolerating homosexuals, atheists, liberals, and others of whom Rev. Falwell does not approve. Rev. Pat Robertson, on whose TV show Falwell spoke, agreed with him.

Earlier in 2002, a former president of the Southern Baptist Convention had called Mohammed a "demon-possessed pedophile." He also asserted that Allah and the Christian God were not the same. His remarks were not repudiated by the new convention president, nor did the remarks prevent President George W. Bush from addressing the group's annual convention.

Meanwhile, the issue of homosexuality is threatening to tear apart the Episcopal Church and the United Methodist Church, and once again to tear apart the Presbyterian Church scarcely 20 years after it was reunified after the schism over slavery more than a hundred years before. The Episcopal Church, too, is rent between "conservative" and "liberal" factions.

In the Catholic Church, the priest pedophilia scandal became, in 2002, the worst crisis in the history of the American church.

Whatever else this crisis shows (besides the fact that some church leaders cared more about image, power, and revenues than about protecting children), it demonstrates the psychosexual immaturity of hundreds of priests who are required to be celibate under the Church's canon law. The outer reflects the inner. The fact that the victims were mostly postpubescent teenagers (though some were children) mirrors the priests' own psychosexual age of maturity. How are such immature priests supposed to lead Christians to spiritual maturity?

The pedophilia crisis is still another example of the Church's intransigence in adhering to the old worldview (remember, per Saint Augustine, sex and the body are bad because sex, even in marriage, transmits the sin of Adam and Eve) despite everything science, including psychology, has discovered over the past hundred years. Regarding canonical celibacy (as distinguished from a genuine inner calling to a chaste life), the Church, like the Pharisees of old, has, in the name of God, heaped burdens on the shoulders of its servants and refuses to lift those burdens (Matt. 23:4).

In short, the Christian Church in the United States, and indeed throughout the world, is in colossal crisis, a crisis that promises to deepen and widen, not go away. No matter the surface issues, the heart of the crisis is between those who still believe in the mythical Sky God and those who do not. The believers, the fundamentalists in each denomination, have a disproportionate influence over the structure of the institutional church. The disbelievers, though some few have influence within the institution, have been the ones more likely to walk away.

In 2002, the U.S. Court of Appeals for the Ninth Circuit (California and other western states) declared the American Pledge of Allegiance unconstitutional because it contained the words "under God" (added by Congress only in 1954). President Bush, who owes his election in large part to fundamentalist Protestants and conservative Catholics, called the court decision "ridiculous" (though it was not ridiculous to Constitutional specialists—wrong, perhaps, but not ridiculous). The *Washington Post*, which accurately represents the mainstream secularized culture of the nation, was blasé. The *Post*, in effect, said the court decision was of minor importance because the phrase "under God" is merely an exercise in "meaningless deism," in other words, a traditional saying that for most people has no meaning.

In the summer of 2002, in response to the so-called Christian Right, the Virginia legislature passed a bill mandating the placement of posters with a certain message in all Virginia public schools. Greeting the children and teenagers in September when they returned to school, the posters proclaimed "In God We Trust." Seventy years ago there would have been no need to enact such a law because a cultural consensus still existed that the mythic Christian Sky God was real. Perhaps by 1954, when Congress added "under God" to the Pledge of Allegiance, doubts were growing. In 1962, as fundamentalists like to put it, the Supreme Court "threw God out of the public schools," and ever since then, even the fundamentalists admit, God has been in retreat. In 1966, a *Time* magazine cover asked, "Is God Dead?"

By 2002, we had apparently reached the point at which God's viability had become dependent on the enactment of laws by such as the good legislators of the Commonwealth of Virginia. When belief in the mythic God has to be legislated and posters with the word "God" put up in the schools, one should realize that not only the battle but the war itself has already been lost.

For most everyone but the fundamentalists, the mythic God of the Bible is dead. Fundamentalist Rev. Tim LaHaye and his coauthor Jerry B. Jenkins have made hundreds of millions of dollars in recent years with a series of entertaining novels based upon their literal (materialistic) interpretation of the symbols contained in Revelation. They believe that God will soon supernaturally intervene on Earth, that good "born-again" fundamentalist Christians like themselves will be "raptured" into heaven (bodies and all), and the rest of the world—nonfundamentalist Christians, nonbelievers, and all those of other faiths—will be subjected to unspeakable horrors for many years until Jesus returns on a cloud to rule for a thousand years. It is pure fantasy. But it is fantasy with a dark side because, as always under the mythic worldview, it projects the anger and vengeance of those who maintain this view onto their mythic Sky God.

Their anger is against all those they envision as deserving horrible suffering and death—all those who hold beliefs other than their own, especially those who hold the rational worldview by which their worldview has been defeated. (That it would now take a massive supernatural intervention by God to save the day is, for all intents and purposes, an admission of defeat.) Mercifully, unlike some of their fundamentalist Muslim counterparts, Christian fundamentalists like Rev. LaHaye are willing to leave to God the dirty work of destroying the heathen and the heathens' civilization.

The "rapture" described by LaHaye and Jenkins once again demonstrates the confusion of the materialistic with the spiritual that is so much a part of mythic consciousness. Christians are "raptured" away from Earth, bodies and all. To where? Presumably, into the Sky God's presence. But how will their bodies survive? After all, physical bodies need oxygen, water, and food and must live within a certain temperature range. Maybe they are to be whisked off to another Earth-like planet. But if so, how will that get them anywhere closer to God than they were here? It is all a confused muddle.

For the rest of the Christian world, God's death is mourned by some and accepted by others. Since most of the Church has been too busy holding onto the past and its thought forms, or battling every new truth that seems to call those thought forms into question, it generally offers no leadership to these bereft souls. They are left to fend for themselves. Having no God to replace the one who has died, they mourn and weep, accept, and, often with great guilt, go on with their lives as best they can. "Whither is God?" cried Nietzsche's madman. "I will tell you. *We have killed him*—you and I. All of us are his murderers . . . God is dead. And we have killed him."[12]

3
Who Was the God Who Died?

The God who has died and for whom the Christian masses now mourn was the ethnocentric Sky God of mythic level consciousness. As American Episcopal Bishop John Shelby Spong has written, "The evidence that God, understood theistically, is dying or is perhaps already dead is overwhelming. I define the theistic God as a 'being, supernatural in power, dwelling outside this world and invading the world periodically to accomplish the divine will.'"[1]

We should all rejoice in the death of this mythic or theistic God because, as President George W. Bush has said, our globally interconnected world cannot any longer tolerate the religious wars, genocides, ethnic cleansings, suicide bombers, hate crimes, bigotry, and similar miseries and atrocities. Most of these, of course, plus other horrors like pogroms, the Crusades, inquisitions, witch and heretic burnings, and the oppression of women and gays, have been perpetrated by people in the name of their various mythic Gods. We are well rid of these Gods, including the Christian Sky God.

However, before we get too excited over the demise of the mythic level in *adults* in Western societies, I want to emphasize that we can never dispense with the mythic level completely. It is a natural stage in the development of consciousness. It cannot be bypassed. It must be lived through, mastered, and then transcended. If we were to go in and deconstruct or destroy a mythic level social, religious, or political structure, chances are not the best that the mythic believers in that structure would then make the effort to transcend the mythic level and enter the rational. They are very likely, given human inertia and laziness, to regress rather than progress.

We see this now in the former Soviet Union, where for decades Communism functioned as a type of mythic religion. Now many in those nations have regressed into the tribalism of Mafia-like gangs and into centuries-old ethnic rivalries. In our own American inner cities, many street gangs are made up of the sons and grandsons of mothers and grandmothers who are pillars in the church. But their offspring, many of whom are fatherless, have regressed into urban tribalism. Afghanistan is another case in point. With the mythic-level Taliban removed from power, there is a huge temptation for the country to descend once again into a land of warring tribes (except in the city of Kabul, where Western-educated civil servants, businessmen, and intellectuals are congregated). Moving whole societies from one level of consciousness to another is an exceedingly difficult task.

To return to the West and Christianity: Now that the mythic God is dead, what about the God of Jesus? Is he dead, too? If he is, then not only the mythic God but Christianity itself is dead. That, fortunately, is not the case.

Two thousand years ago Jesus of Nazareth, a human being (according to the Christian Creed), a Jew, and a mystic who had realized his own divinity, proclaimed a message that he said was the "fulfillment" of the Jewish Law and the Hebrew prophets. His message, which I tried to explain at length in *Putting on the Mind of Christ,* was to manifest, as the goal of human experience, a level of consciousness far above that of his mythic-level contemporaries (and even far above that of today's rational consciousness).

Jesus came as a great light to enlighten the darkness of human consciousness. But, as we know, the darkness heeded him not. The priests (Sadducees) and lay preachers (Pharisees) of his own religion had him killed. After he died, a few of his disciples, mystics in their own right, such as Saint John the Evangelist, tried, as best they understood him, to carry his message forward. They had some minor success, though the message was already beginning to be somewhat compromised as early as the letters of Paul. Whereas Jesus had preached a God of *unconditional* love, Paul, probably because he was unable to make such a radical break with his old beliefs, reintroduced the idea of a God who needed to be appeased. Jesus' words, however, lived on—just as he predicted they would. But by about 150 C.E., Christian understanding of the teachings of Jesus had regressed downward to the mythic level of the general population of the Roman Empire.

Some early Christian communities (generally called Gnostics or seekers of higher knowledge, *gnosis*) did try to hold onto a more mystical, esoteric understanding. But even most of the Gnostics apparently soon regressed into seeking supernatural (psychic) powers and into some wildly unorthodox interpretations of scripture, some of which may have been based upon dubious personal revelations. I say "apparently" because almost all Gnostic writings were destroyed by their Christian opponents. What we have today are the writings of their exoteric adversaries.

Among the intellectuals, Christianity, aside from its periodic saints, stayed at the mythic level until after the time of Galileo. By saints I mean people who have consciously realized their own divinity, such as Francis of Assisi, Teresa of Avila, John of the Cross, and, among Protestants, Jacob Boehme and Joseph Benner. I do not include those who have been declared saints for political or similar purposes, for example, to provide an ethnic role model to Christians in a certain country or because they happened to be martyred for being Christians (Muslims likewise honor their martyrs). John Paul II has canonized hundreds of such political "saints."

It is only today that the masses of Christians are abandoning mythic-level understandings. Since Jesus himself was a great opponent of mythic-level religion—which is why its adherents had him killed—let us examine the characteristics of the God who has died in the light of Jesus' teachings.

The mythic-level God had many characteristics.

1. *The mythic God was a being separate and apart from humans.* The physical plane presents to us the illusion of separateness. Our five senses tell us that we are separate from other people, other living beings, and all else of material creation. Each of us, we suppose, is a separate entity or ego, and at the mythic level (and even the rational and other higher levels), we see God in the same way—as a separate being. Jesus, however, saw and taught otherwise.

Jesus declared, "He who sees me sees the Father." He asserted, "I and the Father are one." He said that the Father was in him and he in the Father. He prayed that we too would come to realize our oneness with the Father as he did. He declared, "Before Abraham was, I AM" (I AM being the Father's sacred name), thus proclaiming his *identity* with the Father. In other words, for Jesus, there was no separation whatsoever between human beings and God. In his mind the two were one. Nor did Jesus acknowledge any separation between human beings.

"Whatever you do to the least of my brethren, you do to me." His opponents, mythic believers, did not understand him. They thought him blasphemous.

2. *The mythic God lived in the sky.* As noted previously, the ancient world thought that heaven was an actual physical place located beyond the vault of the stars. This, they believed, was where people went for an infinite duration of time after they died (if they were spared from hell, which was under the flat Earth). Jesus taught otherwise. "The kingdom of heaven is within," taught Jesus. Jesus taught that the kingdom of heaven was "here," "right now," "at hand," in front of our faces—if only we had eyes to see it, that is, if only we were developed enough in consciousness to realize it.

For Jesus, the kingdom of heaven was not a place. It was a particular level of consciousness, one we now call Christ Consciousness, the highest level of human awareness. We get there by a renewal of our minds, by putting on the mind that was in Christ Jesus. When we reach the kingdom, we can see for ourselves that there is no separation between God and humans, no supernatural world as opposed to the natural world, and no separation between humans.

We are all one. That is the great truth: We are all one. Our human egos, of course, don't like being one with criminals, atheists, drug addicts, heathens, and so forth. Many Christians don't want to be one with Muslims (and vice versa). No, our egos want us to be special. Our egos want us to think we are better than others, that God loves us more than others, that we are "chosen," whereas others are not. But the ego is a liar. God loves everyone exactly the same (though some of us are more open to that love than others). We are all one and, when one has Christ Consciousness, you can see it for yourself.

3. *The mythic God was male and required the subordination of women.* Jesus, although he followed the contemporary fashion of referring to God as Father, taught, as did his disciple Paul

later, that God transcended gender. In the recently discovered Gospel of Thomas, Jesus says, "When the male and female are made one, there is the kingdom of heaven." Jesus did his first miracle at the request of his mother. Jesus had many women disciples. Except for John, only the women stood by him when he was crucified. After his resurrection, he appeared first to Mary Magdalene. Unlike most other Jewish men of his time, he conversed with women often and treated them as equal to men. Since he who sees Jesus sees the Father, we can conclude that Jesus' Father does not oppress or subordinate women.

Jesus actually went further. In many ways he attacked the patriarchal system then in operation. He admonished his disciples to "call no man your father except God." He declared, "If anyone comes to me and cannot hate his own father . . . he cannot be my disciple" (Luke 14:25–26). He flatly disagreed with Jewish divorce law, which allowed the husband, as the "head of the family," to divorce his wife and put her on the streets. One man wanted to be Jesus' disciple but said he had first to bury his father. Jesus bluntly replied, "Follow me and let the dead bury their dead" (Matt. 8:21–22).

To Jesus, seeking the kingdom within was far more important than family obligations or any deference to one's father. Jesus said, "I have come to set a man against his father . . . and a man's foes will be in his own household" (Matt. 10:35–36). Jesus did not see one's relationship with God in terms of following the rules and roles of his patriarchal religion, and he made that clear to the Pharisees and Sadducees, another strike against him in their eyes.

4. *The mythic God was ethnocentric.* As we have seen earlier, the Jewish mythic God was the God of Abraham, Jacob, and Isaac, not of the heathens. But Jesus' God is not. Jesus praised the Roman centurion for his faith, saying he had not come across a faith as great "in Israel." Jesus ministered to the heretic Samaritan woman. Jesus, in the parable of the Good Samaritan, made the

Samaritan the hero and the Jewish religious officials the villains (they refused to touch the man because, under Jewish religious law, that would have made them unclean). Jesus ministered to pagans as well as Jews. In the end, Jesus sent his disciples to all nations. Jesus' God was the true, universal God of all mankind, not the narrow God of any tribe, nation, or religious sect.

After the events of 9-11-2001, patriotic banners sprang up on overpasses over many American interstate highways. Many of them read, "God Bless America." In itself this prayer is fine (except that God always blesses America; it is Americans who sometimes are not open to the blessings). But, I suspect, the banner, to many mythic-level Christians, means "God bless America more than its enemies," or perhaps "God bless America rather than its enemies," or "God bless America and don't bless its enemies," or, finally, "God bless America and defeat its enemies." Only an ethnocentric mythic God, if one existed, would heed the latter prayers. Luckily, one does not exist. Jesus' God, however, loves everyone identically, allowing the rain of His blessings to fall equally on the just and the unjust. But it is our job to open to this love—particularly by raising our consciousness to that of Jesus himself, the level of universal compassion and love.

5. *The mythic God was a God of law.* Under the mythic conception of God, if you obeyed the law and performed the required cultural roles, God would bless you. If you broke the law or did not conform to cultural role expectations, God would get angry and punish you. The God Jesus preached was not like that at all. As Paul later noted in his epistles, Jesus preached liberation from the law, a subject I explored at length in *Putting on the Mind of Christ*. The Pharisees were forever correcting Jesus because he ate with sinners (who were "unclean" under the law of Moses), because he allowed his disciples to work on the Sabbath, and because the disciples failed to wash their hands pursuant to prescribed religious ritual.

Jesus himself ignored the law by speaking to heretics, by conversing with women as if they were men's equals, and in many other ways. Regarding the Jewish dietary laws, Jesus said, "It is not what goes into a man that makes him unclean, but the words that come out of his mouth." For Jesus, salvation was not in following laws of any kind but required a profound change within a person's heart and mind so that the person could "see" the kingdom of heaven here and now.

6. *The mythic God, being a projection of the human ego, had negative as well as positive features.* The God Jesus preached, whom he called "Abba," that is, "Daddy," was a God of love and forgiveness. He was not a human projection but a divine reality that Jesus, as a mystic, had encountered within himself. He was a God who does not judge. He was a God who operates by impartial universal law, sending the rain upon both the just and the unjust. Jesus' God transcends all of the polarities that exist in the realm of space-time, including good and evil. Jesus' God has no negative qualities.

7. *The mythic God was patriarchal and required obedience to his male stand-ins on Earth.* Jesus, as we have seen, criticized patriarchy and the patriarchal system. "Call no man father," he instructed his disciples, "except your heavenly father." The early Christians apparently tried to follow Jesus in this more egalitarian approach. Both men and women were leaders in the early churches. The Christians owned everything in common and gave to each according to his or her needs. Consensus was sought when disagreements broke out such as the one between Peter and Paul over whether Gentile Christians had to obey the Jewish law. Later, when Christianity degenerated back to the common level of consciousness of the times, the church began to set up a more formal patriarchal structure modeled on the family and governmental structures of the times.

Eventually the pope ("papa" or "father") in Rome, citing Matthew 16:18–19, claimed that he, as the successor to Peter as bishop of Rome, was empowered by God to rule over the whole church. Matthew 16:18-19 says, "And so I tell you, you are a rock, Peter, and on this rock I will build my church, which not even death will ever be able to overcome. I will give you the keys to the kingdom of heaven. Solemnly I tell you [plural 'you' in the Greek] this: What you prohibit on Earth will have been prohibited in heaven; what you permit on Earth will have been permitted in heaven."

Whatever the meaning of these verses, they do not refer to the pope. First, in Matthew 16:18, Jesus uses the plural "you" showing that he was referring to all the disciples. Second, Peter was never the bishop of Rome. Rome had a bishop (*epi-skopos*, overseer) only a hundred years or so after Peter's death. Third, for centuries the early Church, even in the West (Cyprian, Augustine), saw Rome as an equal to the other apostolic churches, the churches founded by the various apostles. Augustine interpreted the "rock" as referring to Jesus, not Peter.

The Eastern (now Orthodox) church has never agreed with Rome's interpretation of those verses and, beginning with Martin Luther, Protestants and the Church of England also rejected Rome's view. By the Middle Ages, however, the pope's rule in the West had become monarchical and authoritarian, some popes even asserting authority over secular princes and kings.[2] This reached its height in 1302 when Pope Boniface VIII issued the bull "Unam Sanctam." Based upon a very tortured reading of Luke 22:36-38 (in which Peter, in Gethsemane, tells Jesus that the apostles have two swords handy) Boniface claimed that he, as Peter's successor, had two swords, the sword of spiritual power and the sword of temporal power. Kings, wrote Boniface, derived their power from him.[3]

At least since Moses, mythic believers have looked to the patriarch as God's spokesman on Earth. In Moses' case this is understandable for he did receive genuine mystical revelations on Mount Sinai. But, in the case of the popes of Rome, mystical revelations to them have been few and far between. Contrary to what many mythic-level believers think, popes do not have a special magical pipeline to the Holy Spirit. They, like anyone else, are enlightened only to the extent that they themselves have "put on the mind of Christ," which the vast majority of them have not. Whether they have consciously realized their own divinity or not is a question of fact, not of imagining it to be so. So too is their degree of openness to the Spirit. And, even if a pope has consciously realized his divinity, that does not mean he has all the answers to human problems or human moral questions.

The office of pope is a useful one to the extent it symbolizes the unity of Christians, and perhaps one day, if and when there is actual Christian unity, it might be organizationally useful to a more democratic Christian federation with the pope, perhaps, as president. But despite Rome's interpretation of Matthew 16:18–19, the present institution, especially in practice, is contrary to Jesus' instructions to "call no man your father except God" and to Jesus' instructions to seek the kingdom within rather than in external obedience to law.[4]

8. *The mythic God, because he was a separate being, required that we as supplicants pray to him for our needs and, in response to prayer, he would sometimes intervene supernaturally on Earth.* Again, Jesus rejects the mythic conception. Jesus' God does not intervene supernaturally here on Earth. Jesus was taunted as he hung on the cross because angels did not come to save him. Jesus remained silent. Why do we need to pray to God if, as Jesus assured us, God already knows all our needs? Jesus told us not to worry about what to eat or wear; God will take care of everything. We just need faith. The one thing we should ask for is a realization of the kingdom of heaven within ourselves. ("Seek and you will find; knock and it shall be opened.")

As for miracles, again there was no need for supernatural

intervention. Human beings, provided they have single-minded faith and a high enough level of consciousness, can work so-called miracles themselves. Jesus proved it by doing so, even raising people from the dead. When he worked a miracle, he ascribed its success to the faith of the petitioner, not to God. Jesus also said, "You shall do even greater things." For Jesus, we are the ones who have the responsibility to do the works of God on this Earth, and by our thinking, our actions, and our faith or lack thereof, we are responsible for whatever manifests in our lives, whether miracle or misery.

I am not saying we should never make petitionary prayers to God. God, our own deepest self, always hears our prayers. But we should remember three things: First, God is not a separate being "out there" who listens to our prayers. Instead, God, for us, is our own inner infinite Self. In other words, we are praying to ourselves.

Second, God does not, and never has, supernaturally intervened on Earth. Contemporary philosopher Beatrice Bruteau explains why:

> . . . the Infinite [God] does not "intervene" in the finite. The Infinite as a whole is "exegeted" [manifested, expressed] in the whole of the finite, but the Infinite cannot be a participant in any interaction among the finite beings because that would finitize it. Only finite beings can be agents in finite interactions . . . All finite interactions are defined from particular points of view, and the Infinite cannot take one point of view rather than another. While this may be disappointing, it also relieves us of . . . questions about why the Infinite doesn't intervene [e.g., where was God on 9-11?] in ways we (from our point of view) would like it to do . . .

When we begin correctly to appreciate the nature of the Infinite and the distinction between it and the finite, we may have to give up expecting (requiring?) God to take our part every time we are involved in an interaction that is apt to prove disadvantageous to us. (For popular religion, this is close to being the main item in the job description for God.) But, God is "perfect" (literally, doing thoroughly), that is, whole, not partial, sending sun and rain on both the good and evil, the just and unjust (Matt. 5:45; cf. Deut. 10:17). Many people do not like this; they want a re-active God who operates in terms of the same comparative scales they themselves use (and so protest paying all the vineyard workers the same for different hours, Matt. 20:1-16).

Miracles do occur . . . But our failure (so far) to explain them does not mean that they are outside the laws of nature, the forms of the finite.[5]

All of this does not mean that God is *absent* from our world. As Saint Augustine said long ago, "God is closer to us than we are to ourselves." God is the *withinness* of things, including our own withinness. God is evolving this world *by means of* Creation, including by means of us, using our wills, our intelligence, our emotions, our bodies, and our degree of awareness.

Third, most petitionary prayers are counterproductive because when most people ask God for something—the recovery of health, a new job, a new house—they are saying, "I am lacking health, a new job, a new house; please fill my lack." Your infinite inner self will hear the "I am lacking" and bring more *lack* into your life rather than what you want. You must affirm—in faith—that you already have what you want (Does not the infinite Christ that we are already possess all things?) in order to get it.

9. *The mythic God requires proselytizing and missionary work.* The mythic-level God, because he is the one God, requires proselytizing and missionary work, the conversion of others. Why? Because the one God, as understood at the mythic level, can only be universal when all peoples adopt the doctrines, customs, rules and roles, dogmas and rituals of the particular God. The existence of nonbelievers and believers of other religions is deeply unsettling to the mythic believer. First, because they show that even though the mythic believer's God is universal in theory he is not universal in fact. Second, the others are threatening to the mythic believer's faith. Why?

We must remember that the mythic believer's ego is not very strong. It is only just acquiring dominance in the believer's psyche. So it cannot handle opposing views well. Nor are the mythic believers "inner directed"—seeing their self-worth as God's children, regardless of externals. They are entirely "other directed." They see their self-worth solely in terms of compliance with the external, materialistic roles and rules of their religion. To have others about who disregard those rules or roles, or who have rules and roles of their own, is threatening to the mythic believer's self-worth.

For this reason mythic believers cannot leave others alone. They have to convert everyone so that everyone thinks and behaves like them. Because the proselytism of the mythic believer is fueled by inner insecurity, it has often become violent: Either convert or you may be forcibly converted, attacked in a crusade or other holy war, or burned at the stake. Mythic believers are intolerant—their most annoying and dangerous trait. You may tolerate their religion, but they are not about to return the favor. Because they are intolerant, they are a danger to the rational-level pluralistic state. Politicians who kowtow to them or fund them or encourage them are courting social disaster.

Again, Jesus did not preach a mythic-level God. Time and again he stressed that what was in a man's heart was far more important than following external rules and roles. He encountered people of other religions, Romans, Canaanites, Samaritans,[6] and so forth, but never tried to convert anyone. He preached only that they each go within themselves to find God. True, he later sent his disciples to bring the "Good News" to all nations. But what was the Good News? It was definitely not, at least at the beginning, a new religion with new rules. It was the glorious message that we are all gods, all divine, and that we can consciously realize our divinity by the renewal of our minds.

10. *The mythic God, along with those who go to heaven, lives in an eternal duration of time.* Jesus' God does not live in time. He is not of this world. He is Spirit. Those who realize the kingdom of heaven within are not promised an endless duration of time, either here on Earth or in heaven. They are called to transcend time and to live in what mystics call the Eternal Now. Jesus told many parables about the kingdom that had "vigilance" as their theme. We must always be ready, alive in the moment, living in the now.

The contemporary mystic Eckhart Tolle has written a wonderful book, *The Power of Now,* in which he explores this theme at length, that is, how to let go of time to live as Jesus did, always in the Now. Jesus said, "Before Abraham was, I AM." What did he mean? Did he mean, as the Pharisees thought he did, that the human personality, Jesus of Nazareth, was a couple thousand years old? Obviously not.

Jesus was saying that his True Self, his inner Self, was immortal, that it had never been born and would never die. So he lived always *now.* Anyone who realizes the Christ Consciousness will realize the same thing about themselves. For we are all, as Saint Paul testifies, the Christ. The inner Christ is our real self; our real self is not our human personality. The inner self will never die, and, unlike our personality, it always lives in the now beyond time, in eternity, non-time.

11. *The mythic God existed to satisfy human needs.* As described earlier, for the child aged seven to 14, given the natural egocentrism of that period, God exists to satisfy the child's needs. To the child, that is God's primary purpose, to change broccoli into ice cream if need be. Adults who find themselves in a crisis, such as in a battleground foxhole or an accident or after a cancer diagnosis, usually immediately regress to calling upon God to save them. That's what we have been taught, that, when all else fails, God will swoop down and save us. Except for one thing: God's universe doesn't work that way.

On the contrary, Jesus said that the opposite was true. God does not exist to serve us; we exist to do the will of God. "Not my will but yours be done," he prayed in Gethsemane. "Not everyone who cries 'Lord, Lord,' but those who do the father's will will enter the kingdom." We are here to do the work assigned to us by God, not to aggrandize ourselves and our egos. And, Jesus said, only if the ego (that which separates us from God) dies will we bear fruit abundantly. To live with the mind of Jesus, therefore, we must abandon the self-centeredness and childishness of the mythic level and become mature in the service of God even if it leads, as it did with Jesus, to death on a cross.

12. *The mythic God does not require much responsibility from an individual.* The mythic believer is "saved" by adherence to the law. The Jew has to follow the dietary, marriage, ritual purity, and other laws of the Torah. The Muslim has to follow the five basic rules of Islam: belief in Allah and in Mohammed as his prophet, prayer five times a day, fasting during Ramadan, charity, and a once-in-a-lifetime pilgrimage to Mecca. The Christian has to follow the Ten Commandments plus the rules of the individual denomination, which range from compulsory church attendance on Sunday to the prohibition of dancing. Despite Jesus' constant emphasis on *interior* development, nothing much is required with respect to personal inner growth in consciousness.

Thus the mythic believer is largely outer-directed versus inner-directed, seeing one's self-worth in terms of compliance with external rules versus interior growth. In mythic-level Christianity, Jesus is seen to have redeemed all of human sin so the Christian could be "saved" even if he had been a wife-beater, an adulterer, a thief, or a murderer. As long as he accepts Jesus as his savior, he is saved from taking responsibility for the results of his actions (what a Hindu or Buddhist would call karma). Responsibility is handed over to Jesus.

Jesus, however, taught something different. He was constantly emphasizing the importance of inner growth. Not only was adultery forbidden, but Jesus required that we not lust in our hearts. Jesus said it was what comes out of a man that is unclean, not what goes in. Jesus required a lot more than not murdering; he required that we get to the point where we harbor no anger in our hearts. For Jesus, interior intent and attitude, not external observance, were paramount. Jesus' disciple Paul taught that this interior growth could come about only with a thorough renewing of our mind, that is, a major growth in consciousness. Jesus went to the Cross in faithfulness to the mission God had given him—to preach about the inner kingdom of heaven.

Jesus also taught that we reap what we sow, that if we live by the sword we will die by it, and that we will be held accountable for even our thoughts. In other words, Jesus taught what Hindus and Buddhists call the law of karma, the personal responsibility each individual has for his or her thoughts, words, deeds, and omissions. Jesus taught that we are responsible for our own sins and our own salvation. It is not his responsibility but ours. Jesus did not die to save us from sin. That was a theological interpretation added later by others, and one that directly contradicts what Jesus himself taught.

In short, the God about whom Jesus preached is not at all the same as the mythic Sky God. The Sky God has died because people no longer find him credible, and for very good reasons. He had all sorts of limitations because he was a human projection, and a product of another time and a level of consciousness that has now been superseded. He represented the cutting edge of human spiritual understanding at the beginning of the patriarchal age around four thousand years ago. But now we have outgrown him because our understanding, our consciousness, has further evolved. Jesus and his God, however, have not been left behind. Jesus preached an understanding of God which, for the vast majority of humans, is still in the future, not the past. We will explore that theme in the chapters to come.

4
Can We Replace the God Who Died?

Yes, we can replace the God who died because that God never existed.

He was a projection of the human ego with all the faults of the human ego, including a proclivity toward violence (like roasting certain people forever in hellfire). He was never the real God, but only the God as understood by people who had developed spiritually only as far as the mythic level of consciousness—which was nearly everyone until recent centuries. The real God, the one whom Jesus preached, and the one that we explored at some length in the prior chapter, is not a human projection. He/She is an *experiential reality* whom one can encounter *only* in the depths of one's own being, and only after we have died to ego (the separate sense of self) and been reborn. When we encounter that God in the depths of our being, we also encounter our own true Self, for we, like Jesus, are made of God-stuff. We are one substance with God. We, like God, are infinite consciousness.

The contemporary American philosopher and spiritual sage Ken Wilber does not use the word "God" in his writings because, he explains, the word refers to the mythic God in 99.9% of cases and he doesn't want people thinking in those terms, that is, thinking in the same old ruts. So Wilber uses "Spirit." Likewise, contemporary mystic Eckhart Tolle, another masterful spiritual teacher, doesn't use the word "God" because, he says, the word has been so "misused," by which he also means that to most people it means the nonexistent Sky God. The great twentieth-century American Protestant theologian Paul Tillich called God the "ground of being," echoing Saint Paul's saying that God is the one "in whom we live and move and have our being."

The twentieth-century German theologian Karl Rahner, whose work probably most influenced Vatican II, called God an "incomprehensible mystery" and left it at that. The contemporary French mystic Stephen Jourdain also dislikes using the word "God." Coming from a three-generation family of atheists but enlightened or awakened since the age of 16, Jourdain speaks of encountering within himself what he calls "infinite value." He says that seeing God as a separate being is totally unacceptable. But, he says, "God is me. I can't believe in another God exterior to what I am. On the other hand, the existence of what I call the 'infinite value' appears to me to be obvious."[1] Likewise, the American spiritual teacher Andrew Cohen, who was also raised as an atheist but became enlightened at age 27, does not speak of God, only of an impersonal absolute.

At the highest levels of human awareness, the causal or Christ Consciousness level and the nondual level, the existence of God, as Jourdain says, "becomes obvious." Before that time God is merely believed in (or even not believed in). But the real

God *actually encountered* (which is why God's existence then becomes obvious) in the depths of oneself is so different from the popular mythic God that all of these people who have actually encountered God are trying to find other words to express the experience.

In order to write or speak, we must use language, so we must say something about the encounter with God, the ultimate reality, however inadequate. For me, God is infinite creativity, infinite consciousness or awareness, and infinite intelligence. What we Christians have called God the Father (or Mother) is infinite creativity, the transcendent source of all creation and creativity. The Source is a vast darkness that is nonetheless filled with light and contains the potential for billions of universes and billions of beings.

The great Lutheran mystic Jacob Boehme (1575–1624), who was much admired by John Wesley, the founder of Methodism, describes the act of creation as follows:

> God stirred himself to produce creation. He was desirous of having *children of his own kind*. Creation was an act of the free will of God; God *unfolded* his eternal nature, and, through his active love or desire, he caused that which heretofore had been in him merely as spirit (as an image contained in a piece of wood before the artist has cut it out), to become substantial, corporeal.[2] (Emphases added.)

God's Only Begotten Son is the product of God's "unfolding," of the Father's begetting, the Mother's giving birth. The Only Begotten Son is the Christ of which all humans are members. As Saint Paul said, the whole of Creation groans in childbirth as it gives birth to the sons and daughters of God, that is, to humans enlightened as to their own divinity. Our destiny, then, as God's sons and daughters and members of the Christ, is enlightened awareness or consciousness, infinite awareness or infinite consciousness. Such awareness can only come about in humans because humans are the means by which Creation becomes aware of its divine origin, nature, and destiny and the means by which God knows Herself/Himself. The Son is God's perfect reflection and we—with Jesus and Boehme and all who have realized their divinity—are that very reflection.

God the Holy Spirit is infinite intelligence. Infinite intelligence is the engine of evolution. The Holy Spirit grows us *from the inside*, not only physically, emotionally, and mentally, but also in the evolution of our consciousness, up the ladder of consciousness, step by step, to the realization of our divinity. Infinite intelligence guides our growth into Godhood, just as It did Jesus. That is why he said he must go so that he could send the Spirit upon us. Jesus never meant for us to cling to him, to make him an idol, to cast our sins and responsibilities upon him, to make of him a God (though he knew he was divine). No, he wanted us, and still wants us, to become consciously divine ourselves—that is, to realize that we are already divine.

The Holy Spirit impregnated the "Virgin Mary," the Mother, *Mater*, Matter, the Virginal Material Universe, with the spark of awareness, of consciousness, and then, through the eons, the Spirit has guided that awareness as it has unfolded upward through all the steps of evolution as far as human beings. The Spirit now guides the awareness of human beings on up the ladder of the levels of consciousness until we realize our divinity. The Holy Spirit, as Genesis states, has overshadowed and directed evolution from the beginning. The Holy Spirit will direct evolution to the end—the emergence, through the Holy Spirit, of the *conscious* sons and daughters of God. The Gospel story of the virgin birth is not about the biological birth of Jesus of Nazareth. It is, in story form, a description of the purpose, the means, and the goal of evolution on this planet.

Why a Trinity of Father, Son, and Spirit, of infinite creativity, infinite awareness, and infinite intelligence? Why not just "God"? I prefer the Trinity because, like Augustine, I think the most essential part of Jesus' revelation is that "God is Love." That is the primary Christian revelation, one distinct from (though not contradictory to) the revelations of the other great religions. Love, however, requires both a Lover and a Beloved. In fact, it requires a threesome—the lover, the beloved, and the love itself—a trinity.

The essence of God in the Christian revelation, therefore, is *relationship*. God's nature is relationship. The Father loves by emptying *all* of Himself into His Son the Christ, the Beloved (i.e., all of Creation including ourselves).[3] We, in turn, are led by the Spirit to reciprocate eventually. We, like Jesus, must eventually consciously realize and claim our divinity and then, not thinking divinity anything to be clung to, lovingly empty ourselves in service to others, just as Jesus did.

I give myself completely when I realize that the infinite Christ animates me (and has always done so), when I realize I am not the fictitious separate ego I used to call "I," but that I, like Jesus, am a Christed son or daughter of the God within who lives and expresses through me. When I realize the Christ within myself and give myself away in service to others, then I, too, am Love. Infinite creativity, infinite awareness, and infinite intelligence are related to each other in infinite love. And when we realize our own divinity, we will see that we, too, not only have but *are* all these wondrous things.

God the Father/Mother Source, then, is that principle of infinite creativity from which all of creation continuously springs forth. Spirit is the infinite intelligence that animates creation and grows it from within by the process of evolution. And Christ, in whom all humans participate and of whom all humans are members, is both the firstborn of creation (alpha) and the end of evolution (omega), infinite divine awareness or consciousness.

The contemporary American contemplative Beatrice Bruteau expresses all this quite beautifully. She writes:

> The Trinity is showing itself as world, especially with the characteristic trinitarian trait of living together, symbiosis, mutual indwelling, interacting, sharing. From elementary particles in the atom, through atoms in molecules, molecules in cells, cells in organisms, organisms in societies . . .—all of them being organized as systems—the trinitarian image . . . has been present and growing. "Growing" (from the inside out) is the right word; the Creativity that makes the world is built into the world as its own essence . . . There may not be an *external* Designer and a micro-managing Providence *from the outside* but neither is the world devoid of divinity [for] . . . the world can be regarded as an incarnate expression of the Trinity.[4] (Emphases added.)

In the following chapters we will examine the role of the Spirit (infinite intelligence) in evolution and our own roles as supporting members in the divine cast.

Part II

The Rise of Evolutionary Spirituality

Introduction to Part II

The death of the mythic God is a major factor, probably the main factor, in the decline of Christian churches. Most of those churches are still attempting to preach a mythic God to Christians who have grown beyond the mythic level of consciousness. This decline, coupled with the growing realization that human spiritual growth consists of an inner growth in consciousness, is ushering in a new era in Christianity—the rise of evolutionary spirituality.[1]

Young people now very often label themselves as "spiritual" but not "religious," by which they mean they are interested in personal inner spiritual growth but not necessarily in organized religion. Much as I recognize the importance of organized religious institutions, I consider this a huge step forward because these young people have already come to the realization that spiritual growth is primarily a matter of inner growth, not external observance.

For the Christian Church, this is a challenge at least as significant as the Protestant Reformation and it could, unless Christians generally make a huge effort to increase their level of spiritual awareness, fracture virtually all of the major Christian churches—Catholic, Protestant, and Orthodox. Recent works of many Christian writers, from American Episcopal Bishop John Shelby Spong (author of *Why Christianity Must Change or Die*) to Australian theologian Michael Morwood (author of *Is Jesus God?*) to mystics Andrew Harvey (author of *The Direct Path*) and Walter Starcke (author of *It's All God*) and many others, have been dedicated to the attempt to guide Christianity away from the fallen mythic God. They propose a new understanding of God and of Jesus' teachings and propose a new type of evolutionary or developmental spirituality.

Even though many Christians remain skeptical about evolution, the idea of evolution or "history as progress" is actually a Judeo-Christian concept. The ancient religions of India and Greece saw life as cyclical and history as a series of repetitions in an endless cycle. Judeo-Christianity has always seen history as "salvation history," a history that is going someplace, history as progression toward an ideal end. Christians look forward to the time when the kingdom of heaven will become established on Earth. There have been a variety of expressions of this Christian evolutionary vision throughout the history of Christianity.

One of the most famous expositions of this Christian evolutionary vision was that of Joachim, abbot of the monastery of Fiore in Italy, who lived from 1132 to 1202 C.E. Joachim saw all of history divided into three periods corresponding to the three members of the Trinity. God the Father, the God of law and rules and covenant, oversaw the Age of the Father, the time of the Old Testament. Jesus ushered in the Age of the Son and the establishment of the Church as a human institution (the most important institution in the world in Joachim's time). The Church guided people to God through the observance of external things such as sacraments, rituals, pilgrimages, and moral laws.

But eventually, wrote Joachim, would come the Age of the Spirit prophesied by Jesus—when people would no longer worship God in temples but "in spirit and truth." People would then follow their own inner lights to God and there would be a great flourishing of mysticism.

Joachim, in 1200 C.E., mistakenly thought that the Age of the Spirit was around the corner. So, lest I repeat the same mistake, I am not saying it is around the corner now. I am aware of the enormous work it will take to move billions of humans to higher levels of awareness. But some small beginning of the Age of Spirit does seem to be happening now at the beginning of the twenty-first century.

Millions of people are interested in spirituality though not necessarily in religion. Tens of thousands seem interested in evolving in consciousness into the higher spiritual states preached by Jesus, Buddha, and all the other great teachers of the past. We are now, therefore, seeing the rise of evolutionary spirituality. The second part of this book explores some aspects of this new evolutionary spiritual understanding.

In the introduction to my first book, *Putting on the Mind of Christ: The Inner Work of Christian Spirituality*, I proposed what to many people is a new and startling idea: the proposition that evolution did not cease with the advent of *Homo sapiens* but continues. Based upon the work of pioneers such as child psychologist Jean Piaget, philosopher Jean Gebser, and the American spiritual sage Ken Wilber, I proposed that human consciousness continues to evolve at both the individual and the social/collective levels.

Using the works of many modern psychologists and the works of the great Christian mystics such as Teresa of Avila, John of the Cross, and Meister Eckhart, I drew a map of the development of human consciousness from the archaic consciousness of children to the Christ Consciousness of Jesus of Nazareth. I set forth my view that the "kingdom of heaven" that Jesus preached was the highest level of human consciousness and that the goal of evolution is to bring human beings to that level of awareness so the kingdom of heaven can be manifested right here on Earth.

I also set forth and described nine levels of human consciousness: (1) the archaic consciousness of infants, (2) the magical consciousness of young children, (3) the mythic consciousness of preadolescents, (4) the rational consciousness of teenagers and adults, (5) the vision-logic consciousness of today's consciousness pioneers in the universities and in other fields, (6) the psychic consciousness of beginning contemplatives, (7) the subtle consciousness of advanced contemplatives and mystics, (8) the causal or Christ consciousness of those few humans who have followed Jesus into the kingdom, and (9) the nondual consciousness of identity with God.

People at each level of consciousness have their own world-views. They see and understand the world in a different way from people at other levels. Their values are different. Their conception of God is different. And their behavior, too, is often different.

Each level of consciousness is a holon, a word that means a "part/whole," a part that is also a whole. Each level of consciousness, as one goes up the ladder, includes but transcends the level of consciousness below. The former whole now becomes a part of the wider, more comprehensive whole, just as molecules include but transcend atoms and are themselves included in but transcended by cells.

Moreover, as our consciousness evolves up the ladder of consciousness, we become less and less egocentric and more and more universally compassionate. An infant (archaic consciousness) has what Freud called "primary narcissism." It is not that the infant is selfish in the moral sense, it is just that the infant can recognize only itself, at first not even distinguishing itself from its mother.

At the magical level one identifies with one's family and blood relatives, one's tribe. At the mythic level, one identifies with one's ethnic group, race, nationality, or religious sect. Thus the mythic level is ethnocentric or sociocentric. Each level of consciousness broadens one's concern, compassion, and identification until finally, at the causal or Christ Consciousness level, one no longer identifies with the human personality at all but with Spirit in whom resides the entirety of Creation.

Since writing *Putting on the Mind of Christ,* I have come across the wonderful work of the late American psychologist Clare Graves and his two students Don Edward Beck and Christopher C. Cowan. Dr. Graves's "Spiral Dynamics" is a system of values development roughly parallel to my ladder and that of Wilber's. In fact, Wilber has begun to extensively use the insights of Spiral Dynamics in his own work.

One of the best things about the levels of consciousness as described in the book *Spiral Dynamics* by Beck and Cowan, is that the levels have colors for names: beige, purple, red, blue, orange, green, and so on. This is a nonjudgmental way of describing people's levels of awareness and it avoids some of the complications that can arise from using labels like "mythic" and "rational," words that have different meanings to different people. Another important feature of Spiral Dynamics is that vision-logic consciousness, which is the cutting edge of mass consciousness in the West today, is divided into three separate levels: green, yellow, and turquoise. This makes each level much easier to understand.

The levels of Spiral Dynamics are as follows:

Wilber/Marion	Spiral Dynamics
Archaic	Beige
Magical	Purple
Mythic (early)	Red
Mythic (later)	Blue
Rational	Orange
Vision-logic (beginning)	Green
Vision-logic (middle)	Yellow
Vision-logic (later)	Turquoise
Psychic, Subtle, Causal, Nondual	No color

The Death of the Mythic God

In part 2 of this book I explore the rise of evolutionary spirituality. First, I will explain how Creation comes forth from God, that is, the "involution" that precedes evolution. Then I explore evolution, the return of Creation to God, including the evolution of human consciousness to higher and higher levels of awareness. I explore the levels of human consciousness that are beyond the mythic level beginning with rational consciousness, including the limitations of rational consciousness.

Using the work of Beck and Cowan, I then explore the next highest level of consciousness, the level of vision-logic consciousness, which, as noted, Beck and Cowan divide into three separate levels: green consciousness, yellow consciousness, and turquoise consciousness. Because vision-logic consciousness has been, since the 1960s, the cutting edge of mass consciousness in the West, it is very important for us to understand this level as best we can.

I then go on to explore levels of consciousness that are still best described not by psychologists, but by the contemplatives and mystics of the world's great religions: the psychic and subtle levels of consciousness (which I group together as one level, the subtle). In addition, I attempt to explain some of the realizations and understandings that occur at the higher levels of consciousness regarding such matters as healing, manifestation (the ability to use the higher dimensions of reality to manifest what we want on the physical plane), and karma.

Finally, I deal with the goal of evolutionary spirituality: the realization of the highest levels of human consciousness—the causal (or "Christ") consciousness and nondual consciousness.

5
Involutionary Unfoldment–How Creation Comes Forth from God

In classical metaphysics, both Eastern and Western, the process by which God gives birth to creation (or unfolds the Godhead outward as creation) is usually called involution. I should stress at the outset that this metaphysics is not speculation. It is based upon the actual spiritual experience of thousands of mystics and contemplatives from time immemorial in both the East and West. Some aspects of the unfolding may be speculative but the basic contours are not. They are *data* directly experienced by those who have gone deep within themselves and there have found God.

Source unfolds creation out of itself through five levels of energy vibrations, each of which has many sublevels of vibration.

The closer the vibration to Source the higher and more powerful and more conscious the vibration—exponentially higher
and more powerful and more conscious from one level to the
next highest one. The unfolding of creation, however, goes in
the opposite direction, the vibrations becoming exponentially
less powerful, lower in frequency, and less conscious as creation unfolds downward into matter. The levels are as follows:

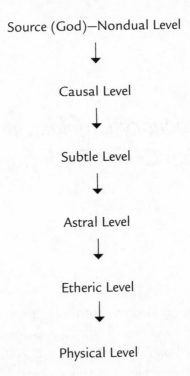

Source (God)—Nondual Level

↓

Causal Level

↓

Subtle Level

↓

Astral Level

↓

Etheric Level

↓

Physical Level

Let us now explore the levels in a bit more detail.

Source (God)—Nondual Level. In the beginning we have
Source, the ground of being, which means that all else depends
upon Source but Source depends upon nothing outside Itself.
God is perceived by those whose consciousness has ascended to
this level as a vast darkness, a void (Saint Dionysios), an empti-
ness (Buddhist *shunyata*), but one which is infinitely full of creative potential and possibilities. God as creator/source is

infinite creativity. The level of Source is called the nondual level because God transcends all the opposites including such opposites as male and female, personal and impersonal, and good and evil.

Causal Level—Mind. The causal level is the first level that comes forth from God, the Christian Only Begotten Son. It is also called Mind (Greek *Nous*). It is the *Logos,* the eternal word, the supreme archetype, the ideal form (Plato),[1] the Christ, the primal principle or design, from which all else of creation will come forth. In the Jewish Kabala this is the realm of the ten primal archetypes, the Sephiroth. In Hinduism it is the realm of Atman, the true higher self, the soul. Because this level of reality is the cause of the levels that will, in turn, unfold from it, it is called the causal level.

Subtle Level. The second level of Creation to unfold is the subtle level. In this level are found the angels and demons (Christianity, Buddhism, Islam, Judaism). Here too is found the Music of the Spheres, the sights and sounds of a "heavenly symphony." The subtle level is one of exquisitely rarified energies, breathtaking beauty, and sometimes an almost cosmic horror. The subtle level is the source of great art, music, mathematics, philosophy, literature, and science via those humans who have been able to tap into it for inspiration.

Astral Level. The third level to unfold is the psychic or astral level. This is the level of dreams, which are made of denser "material" than the phenomena of the subtle plane. Visions are also an astral level phenomenon and, like dreams, they serve as symbolic messengers (*angeloi*) from the soul to the everyday consciousness. The astral level contains all the mental and emotional energies produced by humankind. It includes every kind of thoughtform, both individual and collective, positive and negative.

It is here, for example, that you will find the collective and emotionally charged thought form called the Christmas spirit, a thought form that fades from January through October and then is revitalized each year by millions of human thoughts and emotions as people once again tap into this collective thought form and reinvigorate it.

The astral plane, in a sense, contains a complete record of every thought or emotion ever experienced by a human being (what many have called the Akashic Record). It is also the plane you want to tap into if you want to prophesy, for just as there is a thought of a painting before an actual painting, it is here that human thought and emotion combine to later produce or manifest actions on the physical plane.

Etheric Level. The fourth level to unfold is the etheric. The energies of the etheric plane are almost but not quite physical in density; at least they have thus far eluded the instruments of modern science. Perhaps the most important of the etheric energies for humans is what the Hindus call *prana* and the Chinese call *chi.* The late Indian yogi Gopi Krishna (1903–1984) described *prana* or vital energy as a subtle immaterial substance that pervades the universe and is the cause of all organic activity. It is this vital energy that is made use of by acupuncture and various other Asian healing arts. The human body cannot live without *prana* and it cannot function in a healthy way unless it contains an abundance of this life-giving substance. Oxygen (pure air), fresh fruit and vegetables that still have a lot of life in them, and pure water are among the best sources of prana.

Physical Level. The last of the levels to unfold is the physical realm of space-time, beginning with the smallest subatomic particles—quarks, according to contemporary physics. The quarks combine to form subatomic particles like protons, neutrons, and electrons; these, in turn, combine to make atoms, atoms combine to form molecules, and molecules combine to form cells. Cells combine to make organs and organs to make organisms until we finally get to human beings. Note that each of these levels consists of "wholes" that combine to form greater "wholes." The greater whole is always much more than the sum of its parts and is qualitatively of a different order from the wholes from which it was synthesized. For example, who could have imagined that two atoms of hydrogen and one of oxygen (both gases) would produce something as wondrous as water!

But I have gone too far already in the story of the involution or unfolding of God as Creation, for, with the previous paragraph, beginning with the quarks, I have commenced the homeward journey, the evolution of matter back upward into God, the path of evolution versus involution. Of course, nowhere along the paths of involution or evolution do we ever leave God, for, at base, the whole process is nothing but God. God is the very thing that unfolds and all the levels of both involution and evolution are manifestations of divinity. Everything is divine. Everything is spiritual. Everything, as Saint Francis of Assisi proclaimed in his ecstatic poetry, is shot through with divine light. As Jesus himself said, "The kingdom of God is [always] at hand," but most of us, alas, can't see it.

Even though I have just outlined how God creates this world and operates to evolve it from within, most of the modern sciences have dispensed with God for more than a century now. Some scientists may remain religious in the Sunday churchgoing sense, but they have long ago ejected God from their laboratories and workplaces. The hypothesis of God (the old mythic God) has been found to be of no use to them in their everyday work. Vaccines have been discovered for smallpox, polio, and many other diseases, and astronauts were sent to the moon without any need for recourse to the mythic God. Atheistic leaders have increased the gross national product of China by seven percent or better a year, have built cities, pipelines, and dams, and have fed more people better than ever in China's history—again, with no need for a mythic God. That these things could not have happened without the help of the Infinite Intelligence within the scientists and leaders involved does not seem to have occurred to most of them.

Most scientists do not think that anything exists except matter. Even many biologists think that mind or thought is merely an epiphenomenon of matter, something produced by the action of neurons in the brain. Some imagine that, if they can build a complex enough computer, the computer will actually be able to think, as in artificial intelligence, or AI. Even many psychologists, practitioners of the so-called "science of the soul," think that mental and emotional problems can be explained entirely by recourse to faulty genes or other solely physical malfunctions. Some scientists do acknowledge that nonmaterial things exist—for example, thought—but in their work they ignore everything except the physical because only the physical can be measured.

Nevertheless, the most prestigious of all the so-called hard sciences—physics—has been gradually moving for a century now toward an awareness of the invisible, immaterial realm. The late David Bohm, a brilliant physicist and cosmologist, suggested that the whole of the physical world of space-time (which he called the "explicate order") actually comes forth from an intangible realm that he called the "implicate order." His suggestion is based on many of the findings, implications, and puzzling phenomena that arise from the two great streams of modern physics: relativity theory and quantum mechanics. For nonscientists, including me, Bohm's theoretical work is not easy to follow. But here I try to set forth in as simple a way as I can his idea that space-time is a projection of a higher, simpler dimension of reality.

In his book *Wholeness and the Implicate Order*, Bohm gives the following example of how one reality (as seen in one dimension) can appear as two realities (seen from another, lower dimension): Imagine that you have a clear glass fish tank filled with water. A fish is swimming back and forth in the tank. Then take two TV cameras. One camera focuses on the fish from the front of the tank, the other focuses from the side. Now picture two TV sets in the next room with an audience watching the TVs. One TV shows a fish swimming from a side view. The other TV shows a fish swimming from a head-on or tail-on perspective.

Every time one of the fish moves, the other fish will have a corresponding movement, no matter how subtle. But of course, even though it may seem so to the TV viewers, there is only one fish, not two. On the two-dimensional TV screens it may seem that there are two fish, but from the point of view of three dimensions (which a TV viewer could experience if he or she were to walk into the room with the actual fish tank) there is only one fish. What is one in the third dimension looks like two when seen only in the second dimension.

Bohm, in perhaps his most famous contribution to physics, proposed a similar solution to the Einstein-Podolsky-Rosen paradox. In 1935, the founder of relativity theory, Albert Einstein, together with others, proposed a "thought experiment" called the Einstein-Podolsky-Rosen paradox, which attempted to show the incompleteness of the theory of quantum mechanics. Bohm described a simplified form of this experiment:

> Consider a molecule of zero total spin, consisting of two atoms of spin^2 [one plus, the other minus] ... Let this molecule be disintegrated by a method not influencing the spin of either atom. The total spin then remains zero, even while the atoms are flying apart and have ceased to interact appreciably.
>
> Now, if any component of the spin of one of the atoms (say A) is measured, then because the total spin is zero, we can immediately conclude that this component

of the spin of the other atom (B) is precisely opposite. Thus by measuring any component of the spin of atom A, we can obtain this component of the spin of atom B, *without interacting with atom B in any way.*[3] (Emphasis in original.)

This is true even if atom A is now in Los Angeles and B is now in Paris and A and B are still moving farther away from each other. As soon as we measure any component of the spin of A, the effect upon B is instantaneous. The effect is nonlocal (since A and B are nowhere near each other and only A was measured). It is also instantaneous—that is, faster than the speed of light—because the effect on B happened exactly at the same time as the measurement of A. But, as Einstein showed, nothing *physical* can travel faster than the speed of light, so how can this result be explained?

To solve the paradox, Bohm takes us back to the two fish on the TV screens, which he likens to atoms A and B. Just as any movement of one TV fish instantaneously affects the other TV fish, so too do atoms A and B affect each other even though they are thousands of miles apart. And for the same reason. Just as the fish are two when seen in two dimensions but only one when seen in three, so too, Bohm says, what appears as two distinct atoms in the third dimension is really one reality in a higher dimension.

Mathematically, you need six dimensions to solve the paradox. The supposedly separate atoms are three-dimensional projections into the world of space-time of a six-dimensional reality. This six-dimensional reality is unseen and perhaps unseeable. It is the implicate order from which the "being" of the atoms arises and from the vantage point of which the two atoms are seen as one.

We have been talking about atoms, the conventional "building blocks" of the entire physical universe. Everything physical is made up of atoms. If quantum mechanics implies that the underlying reality of these building blocks exists in a nonphysical dimension, what happens to scientific material-ism, the belief that only the physical universe exists? Quite sim-ple: Materialism is proven wrong—and by science itself. Bohm suggests that quantum theory implies that elements that are separated in space are generally noncausally and nonlocally related projections of a higher dimensional reality. According to Bohm, the physical universe is not only not all there is, but is only one of many possible "explicate" orders that could the-oretically arise out of the hidden "implicate" order.

Bohm goes on to say that what is true of space is also true of time. Time too arises from the implicate order, and discrete events supposedly separated by time are similarly projections of one higher level reality.[4] Finally, Bohm postulates that con-sciousness as well arises from the same immaterial implicate order. Both mind and body, Bohm states, arise from a single nonphysical source, which in its nature is beyond them both. Even separate human beings or human beings as separate from the rest of nature, Bohm argues, are projections into space-time of a single reality beyond space-time. Something invisible, in other words, continually gives rise to the whole of space-time, to all the creatures within it, including ourselves, and to our consciousness as well. That is not far from the words of the Christian Creed: "I believe in God, the Creator (Source) of all things, *visible and invisible.*"

Bohm emphasizes that everything that appears to our senses, including ourselves, is generated by and from, sus-tained by, and will eventually vanish into the vast sea of invisi-ble energy that is the implicate order, an order which is not material because it exists outside the three dimensions of space (and outside time). Bohm then considers what his theory would mean in terms of the evolution of life. He says that the word "evolution" is too mechanistic to describe what is really the successive "unfolding" of living forms. Later living forms (humans) are not "caused" by what went before (apes), except in minor ways, because each species continuously arises more or less independently from the multidimensional implicate order and is a projection of a reality in that order.

In summary, Bohm's work represents a major departure in the science of physics. For several hundred years, ever since Isaac Newton, most physicists have assumed that the material universe constituted the whole of reality and that there were no immaterial or metaphysical (literally "beyond the physical") realities. The metaphysical, invisible world that is affirmed in the Christian Creed ("I believe in one God . . . maker of heaven and Earth and of all things visible and invisible") and believed in by Christians for 1,600 years was rejected as nonexistent.

Bohm, however, suggests that the physical world can no longer be explained by positing only a material universe. There is an "implicate order," he states, which underlies the physical world. This order is nonmaterial, invisible but real. Not only does it underlie the physical universe, but it also in some way actually gives rise to the material universe. The material universe is derived from it. Bohm does not go into any detail in trying to describe this nonmaterial realm, but he does suggest that it may be a realm of many dimensions, a world of vast complexity that science has hardly begun to investigate.

In suggesting a nonmaterial world that gives rise to the physical universe, Bohm is saying what the mystics of every major spiritual tradition—Christian, Jewish, Hindu, Buddhist, Muslim, Neoplatonist, and aboriginal—have been saying for millennia. The world, the mystics say, comes forth from God. It comes forth by steps or stages beginning with what Christians call the Christ, the Word of God who is the firstborn of creation and through whom all the rest of creation unfolds (John 1:3). The Christ is the first "level," or dimension, immediately below God, who is undifferentiated oneness. The Christ then gives rise to lower dimensions, one unfolding out of the other as I described earlier in this chapter.

Some may argue that what I have written in this chapter is the wildest kind of speculation and theory. It is not. That involution is a fact is, as I said, attested to by the mystics of every spiritual tradition. Involution, of course, cannot be proved by the "eye" of the senses. Nor can it be proved by the intellectual "eye" of the rational mind. The truth of involution can only be seen by one's intuitive vision, by what the Christian tradition calls the "eye of contemplation" or the "contemplative gaze." So, if one wants to check the truth of involution, one need only go deep enough within to see it. It is, however, encouraging for the future that scientists like Bohm are discovering that there is a nonmaterial realm from which the universe arises.

6
Evolution–The Path to Conscious Divinity

The standard theory of evolution that has been with us since shortly after Darwin states that life on Earth has evolved through two mechanisms: natural selection and random mutation. A possible example of natural selection may have occurred some 65 million years ago when, most scientists believe, a giant asteroid hit the Earth with the result that conditions for life on Earth were drastically changed for many years. The dinosaurs may have died out because of these new conditions, while small mammals, who adapted to the new conditions (or at least survived them), were then able to flourish. Smaller examples of natural selection happen all the time: A fertile area suffers erosion and soil depletion and turns into a desert, or a temperate area suffers a prolonged cold spell, both of which require the organisms living in such areas to adapt to the new environments.

Random genetic mutation, on the other hand, occurs in all living organisms. Most mutations are harmful or of no importance. But some allow the organisms to adapt better to changing environmental conditions and so cause the species to evolve in a new direction.

In the 1990s, those who opposed evolution resurrected a two-hundred-year-old theory called "the proof of God by the argument from design" to refute evolution. A leading proponent was Michael Behe, professor of biochemistry at Lehigh University in Pennsylvania, who published *Darwin's Black Box* in 1996. In that book he argued that complex living organisms or systems could not be accounted for by random mutation. Others, arguing from the mathematical laws of probability, maintained that four billion years was nowhere near enough time for life to evolve upon Earth simply by random mutation and natural selection. Life, they said, had to be the result of intelligent design, which proved that there was an Intelligent Designer, that is, God.

Others argued a variation of the design argument called the "anthropic principle." Life would not exist upon Earth, they argued, if any one of hundreds of variables were even slightly different from what it happens to be: if the Earth were colder, if the Earth were hotter, if the Earth rotated faster, if the rainfall were different, if the Earth were closer to or farther from the sun, if there were not abundant water, if the air had insufficient oxygen, and so forth. As it is, they averred, the Earth, like Goldilocks's bed, was "just perfect," showing that the Earth had been designed from the very beginning to produce human life.

Most scientists were not convinced by the arguments of these "new Creationists" (though some American school systems have been). Kenneth Miller of Brown University refuted the arguments of Behe in his 1999 book *Finding Darwin's God*. Others pointed out that the part of the argument based on mathematical probabilities was flawed. Others argued that the "proof from design" was circular and thus begged the question. These arguments between scientists and creationists continue into the twenty-first century. We need not, however, get into them in this book beyond saying that a belief in an *external* Designer is a mythic-level belief that needs to be left behind.

Shall we then be content with "randomness" and "chance"? Beatrice Bruteau writes:

> The world has been presented to us as a great machine, something dead and in itself meaningless, something that rolls on relentlessly, ruthlessly, incapable of sensitivity or significance. It starts from a fluke of a fluctuation and thereafter operates by chance and necessity. It's not trying to accomplish anything, it has no purpose, and we human beings have no special place in it. We are simply an accident, an improbable accident, and our request for meaningfulness meets with no reply from the universe.[1]

Unlike some scientists, who seem content with this description of the meaninglessness of life, most people will never be so content. Most people will not live a life of no meaning. We would commit suicide individually or en masse by destroying the planet rather than submit to such impoverishment of spirit (and some might say that is exactly what we are doing). "Where there is no vision the people perish," warns Proverbs (29:18). That is what gives the creationists their power, no matter how faulty their scientific reasoning may be.

What I am proposing, like Bruteau and many others, is that the universe is a manifestation of God, God's "son" in

Christian mythology. Bruteau says that it is the nature of God to be all He/She can be, that is, to express Himself/Herself in every conceivable way, to try out every potentiality, to realize every possibility—including every *finite* possibility. Like the Source, creation is itself infinitely creative.[2] Creation is self-creating, ever expressing its beingness in every conceivable way—even in genuinely novel ways and species that have never arisen before. Permeated with infinite intelligence, the universe is a self-evolving organism. Both randomness and natural selection are means to such self-expression and self-evolvement. The universe is the "living God" in action.

Bruteau again:

> My point, addressed to all those who feel that modern science has stolen their God or made God unnecessary, is that this is not so at all. Our sciences are revealing God, showing "how God does it." And it all has to be done under the conditions of finitude . . . These will include both randomness and determinism, which religious people often yearn to reject. But these should not dismay us. Randomness and determinism are two of the ways you get creativity in the conditions of finitude. They provide for novelty and stability.[3]

A self-evolving universe needs both novelty and stability. It achieves this by growing through holons. "Holons," a word coined by writer Arthur Koestler (1905–1983), is a "whole" which is also a "part." A quark is a whole but is part of an electron. An electron is a whole but is part of an atom. An atom is a whole but is part of a molecule. A molecule is a whole but is part of a cell. A cell is a whole but is part of an organ. An organ is a whole but is part of a human being. The universe evolves by building ever more complex holons built up by the *relationship* between lesser holons.

Why holons? Because they provide both stability and novelty and allow evolution to proceed rapidly. Koestler based his idea of holons at least in part upon the "parable of the watchmakers," as created by Nobel Prize-winner for economic sciences Herbert Simon (1916–2001): There were two watchmakers, Hora and Tempus, and each made watches with a thousand parts. Both were very busy, their phones constantly ringing. Eventually, Hora prospered but Tempus went bankrupt. Why?

Tempus made his watches one part at a time. Every time he had to answer the phone the watch fell apart and he had to start over. But Hora divided the watch into subwholes. Each watch was made of ten components each having a hundred pieces. And each of the components was made of ten subcomponents of ten parts each. All of these subwholes could stand on their own, so when Hora answered the phone, none of the completed subwholes fell apart. Hora, unlike Tempus, worked with holons, parts with their own inner stability and wholeness.

Novelty comes in a different way and is best seen in nature, not in human-made articles like watches. Hydrogen and oxygen, two holons, combine to produce water—an astonishing novelty considering its origin in two gases. Sodium, a poisonous metal, and chlorine, a poisonous gas, combine to make sodium chloride, table salt, a staple of human life. Combining holons, which are stable wholes in themselves, produces all sorts of surprising novelties, the new whole being much more than the mere sum of the parts.

Nor does evolution stop with human beings, for human consciousness also evolves. We have already traced the evolution of human consciousness through four stages: the archaic consciousness of infants, the magical consciousness of young children, the mythic consciousness of preadolescents, and the rational consciousness of most Western adults. As the American philosopher and mystic Ken Wilber has said repeatedly, each of these stages can be seen as a holon, a whole that can stand on its own but is a part from the vantage point of the next higher level of consciousness. Each new level is indeed novel, a surprisingly new and creative development that could not have been predicted by a mere examination of the component parts.

It is also because all the levels of consciousness are holons that we cannot skip levels of consciousness in our own development any more than nature could skip from an atom to a cell, bypassing the molecule. Each level is a whole, a stable component that is a necessary prerequisite to the emergence of the next highest level. Without molecules, there would be no cells. Without mythic consciousness, rational consciousness cannot emerge. This is one reason why it is so important to allow children to develop at their own natural pace and not try to force them prematurely into levels they are not yet ready for as, unfortunately, so many parents and educators try to do today with disastrous results in both elementary and secondary education.

Another force that guides evolution is what the British biologist Rupert Sheldrake calls "morphic resonance."[4] One of the things that nature does, if it has once done so successfully, is to repeat what works, over and over. Nature, to some extent, retains stability by getting into a rut and staying there. Sheldrake gives the example of the form of complex protein molecules. Such molecules, theoretically, could have formed in a million different ways. But, when they first emerged in the course of evolution, they emerged in just a few basic patterns. In the millions of years that have passed since then these are the patterns that nature has used. The same is true of countless other aspects of evolution.

This works against further creativity, of course, but it stabilizes the holons—whether molecules or organisms or levels of consciousness—that have so far successfully developed. Nature, in a sense, "remembers" what works and what doesn't work and saves itself the trouble of making the same mistakes a trillion times over. Even though morphic resonance works against creativity in limiting further wild experimentation, it helps creativity in another way.

Sheldrake noticed, based upon many studies and experiments that had been done with rats, that if you train a group of rats to do a certain task, subsequent generations of those rats will learn the same task more quickly. Also, the more rats you train, the more quickly later rats will learn the task. Even rats that are descended from untrained rats will learn faster; even rats thousands of miles away will learn faster.

In other words, once a task has been learned anywhere in the process of evolution and becomes a "habit," this habit is passed to others and, rather quickly, becomes the habit of all. A conclusion one can make from this is that whenever any discovery or invention or breakthrough (whether in science or consciousness) is made anywhere in the world, the faster others will be able to master that discovery, invention, or breakthrough, and the more people who do, the faster subsequent generations will learn the same.

But where is this memory stored? If it were stored within the individual organism—within our (or the rats') brains or DNA—would it not perish when the individual organism died? Sheldrake proposes that memory is stored in "morphic fields," which are outside what we ordinarily consider space-time[5] and which influence the development of forms, including organisms and fields of consciousness. The information in morphic fields is perhaps communicated to us by means of the brain or the DNA, the brain or DNA acting like a TV set picking up electromagnetic waves of information from elsewhere. Morphic fields are why the levels of consciousness through which most of the human race has so far developed—archaic, magical, mythic, and rational—are now relatively stable. They have become the ingrained developmental habit of the species.

Wilber notes that archaic consciousness has been around since *Homo sapiens* first emerged, magical consciousness for about thirty thousand years, and mythical consciousness for about three thousand years. Rational consciousness has been with us on a widespread basis for only three hundred years or so. Because of morphic resonance, Western children, if properly nurtured, can move through all these levels in perhaps 15 years—levels that took humanity hundreds of thousands of years to first navigate. (Western children now quickly recapitulate these levels of consciousness just as our bodies recapitulate the entire process of Earthly biological evolution in the womb.)

Future levels of consciousness, however, have not yet been made into a habit. So they are much more fluid. No one, for example, knows what this planet would look like, or what our institutions or culture would be like, if the majority of adult humans were at the causal level of consciousness. Only time and our own developmental contributions will determine the future. This space-time universe is self-evolving and we human beings (as far as we know) are the prime agents of that evolution.

Where is evolution going? What is the point of it all? Saint Paul gave us the answer when he wrote that the whole of Creation is groaning in labor in order to produce the sons and daughters of God. God is evolving sons and daughters, people who *consciously realize* their own divinity and thereafter become conscious cocreators with God of the future. Normally, it takes hundreds if not thousands of lifetimes for a human soul to realize its divinity, to realize that it is one with the Creator (as Jesus did) rather than merely a poor put-upon creature.

The whole of the physical space-time universe is designed to *speed up* this evolutionary process, not by an external divine designer but by the divine creativity that is the very essence or "withinness" of the universe itself.

The evolutionary process is sped up by placing humans in an environment that reflects back to them their own consciousness and that manifests relatively quickly the results of their choices. The practice of spirituality is meant to speed up the process even more. All spiritual "technologies"—revealed scriptures, meditation, rituals, fasting, almsgiving—are meant to speed up the evolutionary process, to move human consciousness to higher and higher levels. We are all of us moving toward the conscious realization of our own divinity. The only difference is that some of us are further along than others and some work harder at it than others. But we are all on the train of evolution and the train is moving.

Some day all of us will have the consciousness that was in Jesus himself (Phil. 2:5). Evolution, someday, will bring the kingdom of God upon Earth, provided of course that we don't use our free wills to derail the whole process, at least in this particular solar system.

Now that I have sketched out the general framework of evolution, let us return more specifically to the levels of consciousness by which we ascend the ladder into conscious divinity.

7

Reason Run Rampant

Although there have been for millennia people with rational consciousness (one thinks of Plato, Cicero, Confucius, and many other ancients), Western culture as a whole did not begin to embrace rational consciousness until the Protestant Reformation and the Renaissance. The Age of Reason began to triumph politically with the French and American Revolutions of the eighteenth century. It began to triumph economically with the industrial revolution and educationally with the establishment, in the early nineteenth century, of universal public education. Today the rational level of consciousness dominates almost every area of human endeavor except in certain religious groups that refuse to let go of the mythic level.

As I mentioned in the introduction, one of the reasons why I have spent so much time in this book differentiating rational from mythic consciousness is because so many genuinely religious people, people who are sincerely seeking God, are still stuck somewhere between these two levels, one foot in the mythic level and one foot in the rational. President George W. Bush seems a perfect representative of so many others. When he calls his "war on terrorism" a contest of good versus evil, he is thinking at the mythic level where the world is divided between good guys (always people like us) and bad guys. But when he calls his war a contest to preserve civilization, he is thinking at the rational level. "Civilization" is a universal concept that goes beyond ethnocentric or sociocentric concerns.

United Methodist theologian James Fowler, who is head of the Center for Ethics and teaches at the Candler School of Theology, both at Emory University in Atlanta, studied developmental psychology at Harvard in the early 1970s. At Harvard he was influenced by the work of Jean Piaget (childhood consciousness development), Erik Erikson (eight stages of psychological development from infancy to old age), and Lawrence Kohlberg (stages of moral development). Dr. Fowler made the field of Christian religious development his own field of research and study. In 1982 he published his landmark book, *Stages of Faith: The Psychology of Human Development and the Quest for Meaning,* which is now in its thirty-fifth printing.

His work, which is based upon many empirical studies, is important because it shows that most American Christians, like President Bush, are somewhere between the mythic and rational levels of consciousness.[1] Fowler's stage of "mythic/literal faith" pretty much tracks what I have written earlier concerning the mythic level of consciousness. But then he goes on, based on his research, to break the rational level into two distinct levels.

The first of these levels he calls "synthetic/conventional faith," which he says normally arrives in adolescence with the development of what Piaget called formal operational thinking (the ability to think about thinking). Fowler notes that people with synthetic/conventional faith (not only adolescents but also most American Christians) are deeply concerned about what others think about them. They want an identity that fits into the community or group to which they belong. They want God to be their friend, to care for them personally, to value them, and to anchor their identity.

Notice that the person at this level is still very other-directed versus inner-directed. They care most about what their peers say or think about them. They want to "fit in" and attend church primarily as a social ritual, one affirming their value as a "good person." God's job, too, is to affirm their value. They are not as rigid, aggressive, or literal minded as people at the mythic level, but neither do they have much creative ability. They go along to get along.

Fowler says that some American Christians begin to graduate into the second level of rational consciousness, what he calls "individuative/reflective faith" (when individuals begin to think for themselves), as early as age 17, but that most don't complete the passage until their mid-20s, some not until their late 30s—and some never. Basically, people at this level begin to think for themselves and cease to engage in group-think. They become more inner-directed and now want to belong to a group or church only if they believe the group or church authentically reflects their values. They move resolutely away from defining the self in an ethnocentric or sociocentric manner and become more universal in their thinking. Their God is now a truly universal God who cares for all human beings. Despite all these advances, people at this level can be rigid and ideological in their thinking. They have definite opinions about a host of matters and their identities are wrapped up in these beliefs.

At this stage the ego is very strong. People are ruled by ideas and very often suppress sexual expression and aggression.

Meaning is sought in individualistic terms, as in personal achievement versus going along with the crowd. If the person is a scientist or an entrepreneur, the laws of science and economics can be manipulated for personal gain. The world is a pool of resources to be exploited, and so are other people, as reflected in the label of "human resources" in use in governmental and corporate human resource departments.

People are seen primarily in terms of economic winners and losers. The world is divided between have and have not countries. Competition is seen as an important value. Everything becomes a question of competing and fighting—fighting economic competitors; fighting for political office; fighting cancer, diabetes, AIDS, and heart disease; fighting drugs; fighting racism and sexism; fighting for family values; fighting terrorism; fighting traffic; fighting for the American way of life; fighting, fighting, endless fighting. (And people wonder why they are so stressed!)

As everyone who has paid any attention to the world environmental crisis knows, the planet is now suffering from the excesses of the rational level. Reason has run rampant. Earlier we saw how the rise of the ego to supremacy in the psyche brought about the suppression of women, gays, emotions, sexuality, and the body. We also saw how these suppressions affected the whole of culture and society. The ego became a tyrant, almost always a patriarchal tyrant because the ego was seen as male.

Nature too was suppressed. It was seen not as something humans were part of but as something external to humans, the only value of which was exploitation. Rain forests have been destroyed. Billions of tons of toxic chemicals have been dumped on farmland and into lakes, streams, and rivers. Mammal and fish species have been driven to extinction or close to extinction. The biodiversity of the world's organisms has been drastically reduced. Millions of animals have been killed for their fur or for sport. Millions of others have had their habitats destroyed.

Commercialism and unbridled capitalist competition have paved over millions of fertile acres of land for parking lots, strip malls, fast-food outlets, and other forms of ugly suburban sprawl. Professional workers have been locked into glass boxes where they work cut off from nature, not even able to open a window. It is cheaper and more efficient that way. Chemicals have poured out of smokestacks to later precipitate as acid rain that has destroyed forests and lakes and the species reliant on those habitats. A huge ozone hole has opened over the Earth, endangering people with cancer from ultraviolet rays. The whole globe may be dangerously warming from the buildup of automotive emissions and other greenhouse gases, but Americans have spent billions on gas-guzzling SUVs that Congress has exempted from mileage standards.

Economics overshadows virtually everything from Internet pop-up ads to the length of the college sports season to the naming of sports stadiums. Nor is the commercialism confined to America. The textile industry in Zambia, for example, has been destroyed at the cost of more than forty thousand jobs by the importation of tons of secondhand clothing given by naïve Americans to charities (which sell them to exporters for a profit). Giant banks charge consumers exorbitant credit card and other fees and then use the money to swallow up competitors, each hoping to achieve global importance and reach. Even charities such as the United Way have gotten onto the gravy train of greed, often paying their executives annual salaries of hundreds of thousands of dollars gleaned from the contributions of ordinary working people.

Many of rationalism's successes have also brought huge problems. The eradication of smallpox and other diseases has brought exponential increases in the world's population with millions of people crowding into the slums of cities in the lesser developed countries. The population increase has put huge strains on the planet's natural resources such as timber and water. Consumer goods in America and Europe have been kept inexpensive by shifting millions of jobs from the developed countries to the lesser developed countries, where people are being exploited by almost slave wages and with little heed for the environment or worker safety.

Neither the people who have lost their jobs nor the newly exploited people have been seen as people at all. Labor has often been seen as just another commodity to be used for the aggrandizement of industrialists, corporations, and stockholders. Increasingly, a smaller percentage of the workforce belongs to labor unions as corporations seek to maximize profits by reducing wages and jettisoning pension and health benefits. The gap between the rich and poor grows within countries and between countries. Los Angeles, some say, is now becoming a "third world" economy—a few very rich and millions of working poor. Washington, D.C., and other American cities are headed in the same direction.

Because science discovered that "it could be done," nuclear power plants have been built in many nations; the waste from these plants will remain radioactive for hundreds of thousands of years. Likewise, new kinds of ever-more-terrible weapons have been invented and trillions of dollars have been spent by the United States alone to arm itself and whatever countries it has favored at a given time. Other nations have done the same. Today there could be as many as ten nations with nuclear weapons. Similarly, because it could be done and a profit could be made, genetic engineering and irradiation have been introduced into the food supply with little thought for long-term consequences.

Science has evolved into thousands of specialties, each one studying a small portion of the physical world. Every specialty has its own jargon and scientists from one field often cannot understand scientists from others. Everyone is studying a part and scarcely anyone the whole. Most of our scientists and doctors are lost in the trees and missing the forest just when we need global leaders and thinkers. As for the nonphysical world of spirit, that is generally neglected by science altogether (even in sciences such as psychiatry) because it cannot be measured by the five physical senses and the instruments that are their extensions.

The entire world is now reeling from the excesses of the rational-level mind. Many people wonder whether the human race can even be saved. That is how bad it has gotten. Most of the world's leadership (and this is very typical of the rational level) think that the solution is more of the same. More, more, more. More suburban sprawl, more malls, more dams, more chemical factories, more fertilizer for farms, more oil drilling, more superhighways, more supertankers plying the seas, ever greater gross national products for every nation, ever greater retail sales, housing starts, military expenditures, and trade levels.

General Motors, for example, predicts that between 2002 and 2012, the Chinese will purchase 18 new cars for every 11 bought by Americans. And Indians will buy 9.[2] It seems clear that the present system of more and more cannot go on indefinitely, probably not even for a few more decades. Massive changes are needed in thinking, policies, technologies, and lifestyles.

The problem is that very few people on this planet *have* a global perspective. They are not nearly developed enough in consciousness to have one. They are ruled by their own narrow needs. Brazilians are slashing and burning the rain forests to get more farmland for Brazilians; Japanese are hunting whales because the Japanese people have traditionally liked whale meat; Nepalese are cutting down everything that grows for firewood even though the melting Himalayan snows will then erode the stripped land; poachers kill elephants and rhinoceroses for the supposed aphrodisiac in their tusks and horns; and the United States spends hundreds of billions of dollars every year on weapons so it can be seen and feared as "The Superpower." President Bush's Deputy Secretary of State Richard L. Armitage has boasted, "We've got more influence, power, prestige, and clout beyond any nation in the history of the world." Ego triumphant. Madness and insanity.

Eckhart Tolle, noting that we humans killed 100 million of our own species in the twentieth century and that we are now in the process of destroying the planet upon which our lives depend, observes, "Humans are a dangerously insane and very sick species. That's not a judgment. It's a fact."[3] And it is the tyranny of the rational male ego that is the culprit here, the cause of all this imbalance. The development of the separate individualized ego was a colossal achievement for human consciousness. But ego has now become the principal obstacle to further human progress.

Add to all of this the fact that spiritual teachers such as Tolle are explicit that it is the rational mind itself, now so highly developed in the West, that is the single biggest obstacle to enlightenment or higher consciousness. Tolle says, "Thinking has become a disease. Disease happens when things get out of balance . . . The mind is a superb instrument if used rightly. Used wrongly, however, it becomes very destructive . . . You believe that you are your mind. This is the delusion. The instrument has taken you over."[4]

Clearly, we must move as many people past the rational level as fast as possible into higher, more "worldcentric" levels of consciousness or we are lost. The world can no longer afford to operate even at the rational level—not if it is to survive. And there may not be much time left.

Now let us examine the next level: vision-logic consciousness.

8
Vision-Logic–The Consciousness of the Greens

In *Putting on the Mind of Christ* I wrote a short chapter describing in the most general way the highest of the mental levels of consciousness, vision-logic consciousness.[1] At vision-logic consciousness the rational ego is still supreme. The person still identifies the "self" with the mind. But the mind has now developed to the point where it has a wider worldview.

Forsaking ideologies, the person can now understand things from many different perspectives. The person can appreciate the "context" of things and realizes that everything and every person exists and operates within a context, often a culturally distinct context. The same God, for example, is now seen as being worshiped in many different ways by people of varying nationality and tradition. The "contexts," too, exist within contexts. Just as a word may take its meaning from a sentence, the sentence from the paragraph, the paragraph from the page, the page from the chapter, and the chapter from the book, cultural contexts can go on like this forever.

The same is seen of all the sciences. It is not enough to understand just the parts. Wholes must be studied—whole organisms, whole ecosystems, whole societies, whole historical eras, and whole institutions. Life needs to be seen and appreciated in all its pluralism and diversity. We must be careful not to judge other people based upon superficialities or mere differences in race, gender, nationality, religion, or sexual orientation. All persons, cultures, and religions need to be treated with respect.

Vision-logic consciousness will be readily understood by anyone who has attended a major American university in the last 20 years because these are the values now treated in many of the universities as the most important: pluralism, diversity, globalism, including the global environment or "context," multiculturalism, holism, and the importance of contexts in general. Oppressive pathological hierarchies are scorned and correctly seen as aberrations, reason become tyrannical. They are pathological because they are "dominator" hierarchies wherein some human beings lord it over and oppress others. The pedophile scandal in the Catholic Church is just one symptom of the illness of an institution governed by a pathologically oppressive patriarchal hierarchy that has little use for women, gays, sexuality, the body, or even, at times, human nature, even the human nature of Jesus.

Although many researchers have described the vision-logic level of consciousness, perhaps the best description—because it is the most fine-tuned—has been in the work of psychologists Don Edward Beck and Christopher C. Cowan, both of whom, as I mentioned previously, were students of the late American psychologist Clare Graves. As I discussed, in their book *Spiral Dynamics* Cowan and Beck divide the vision-logic level of consciousness into three separate levels, which they label with the colors green, yellow, and turquoise.[2]

The first level of vision-logic consciousness to emerge is the green. It is the only level to date to emerge on a mass basis. The rise of green consciousness in Europe and America in the 1960s was accompanied by the rise of the environmental movement and of Green political parties both in the United States and even more so in Europe. Former Vice President Al Gore, who wrote a book on the need for environmental protection, is a fine example of a person with green consciousness. Philosopher/mystic Ken Wilber, who has made great use of the work of Cowan and Beck, succinctly describes green consciousness:

> *Green: The Sensitive Self.* Communitarian, human bonding, ecological sensitivity, networking. The human spirit must be freed from greed, dogma and diverseness; feelings and caring supersede cold rationality . . . Emphasis on dialogue, relationships . . . Reaches decisions through reconciliation and consensus . . . Strongly egalitarian, anti-hierarchy, pluralistic values, social construction of reality, diversity, multiculturalism, relativistic value systems . . . Shows a greater degree of affective warmth, sensitivity and caring, for earth and all its inhabitants.[3]

Green consciousness is also very much concerned with righting the rational/male imbalance that has become so dangerous to the health of society and the planet by restoring the feminine to its proper role within individuals, the family, and society. "Feminine," of course, includes not just gender (restoration in this sense reversing centuries of patriarchal repression of women), but also the body, emotions, sexuality, and an appreciation of nature, Mother Earth (Gaia Herself). So it is again no coincidence that, along with the environmental movement, the rise of green consciousness has also ushered in an era of greater sexual freedom in general, and gender role freedom in particular—feminism and the liberation movements for gays, bisexuals, and transgendered persons.

The 1960s marked the beginning of the huge cultural shift from rational (orange) to vision-logic (green) consciousness, both in the United States and in Europe. That shift is still gaining momentum. Conservatives such as sometime American presidential candidate Pat Buchanan and columnist George Will and neoconservatives such as Norman Podhoretz generally think the 1960s produced a great cultural disaster rather than a liberation into a higher level of consciousness. That is not the case. Granted, the 1960s were a cultural disaster for the patriarchal Ozzie and Harriet rational-level culture of big government, big labor, big industrial corporations, and big centralized religions with their entrenched systems of racial segregation, sexism, homophobia, exploitation, and so forth. But the demise of that culture is a plus, not a minus.

The green revolution is now permanent at most major American universities, in the European Union, at the United Nations, and increasingly elsewhere. It is the impetus behind the protests that are besieging the World Bank and the International Monetary Fund (IMF). The World Bank and IMF are largely symbolic, and the symbolism is much the same as Al Qaeda's targeting of the World Trade Center: The real objects of the protests are the multinational corporations that, in effect, now rule most of the world and that are often interested in just two things: the maximization of their executives' compensation and the maximization of shareholder returns—a purely orange value system.

Nevertheless, the critics of green consciousness have some valid points. As I mentioned earlier, green consciousness is still a mental-level consciousness and so by definition is an obstacle to higher consciousness or enlightenment. Green consciousness also has other limitations and downsides.

Perhaps the finest critique of the limitations of green consciousness has been provided by Ken Wilber in his book *Boomeritis*. Many university teachers of cultural and literary studies, says Wilber, have arrogantly proclaimed themselves to be morally superior to all previous generations because they themselves are "pluralistic" and previous generations were not. Down with all dead white Western heterosexual males! That this includes geniuses such as Plato, Thomas Aquinas, Michelangelo, Shakespeare, Newton, Jefferson, and Edison is beside the point. In the minds of some academics, these men were not pluralistic, so they are inferior to today's academic critics.

Another aspect of this arrogance is the proclamation by many "deconstructionists" that there are no facts, *only* contexts—and every context is produced by some type of oppressive power hierarchy. There also are no values because one context is as good as another—it just depends upon who has the power to impose his context on others. All hierarchies are out. No civilization is better than any other. No values are superior to others. In other words, absolute pluralism and relativism. That these green thinkers make their own relativism absolute does not seem to concern them. They don't seem to see the contradiction. Nor does the fact that nature is filled with *natural* rather than *pathological* hierarchies—from quarks to atoms to molecules to the levels of consciousness—seem to deter their total rejection of all hierarchies.

As Wilber has noted (on his website, www.shambhala.com), the destruction of the World Trade Center has caused a real crisis for many greens. Since no values and no culture are any better than any other, how can one condemn the terrorists who committed this atrocity? Isn't fundamentalist Islam just as good as liberal democratic pluralistic America? How can we create a judgmental hierarchy and rate the one system of beliefs and values as any better than the other? This was the dilemma many greens faced after 9-11. Furthermore, since greens believe in sending "love and light" to everyone and are squeamish about confrontations of any sort, they can almost never bring themselves to support military action of any kind. Many, in fact, dislike the military in principle as an oppressive institution of no value at all.

This is the kind of confused thinking that results from not knowing—or refusing to acknowledge—that there are indeed different levels of human consciousness. There is a *natural* hierarchy of levels of consciousness, each one transcending and including the one below. The green level of consciousness, even though many greens hate to admit it, is, as Wilber says, a very elite level of consciousness. That is a fact. People like the Taliban and Saddam Hussein have a much lower level of consciousness and a whole different value system.

Beck and Cowan would place the Taliban and Hussein at the "red" level of consciousness, which they describe as a level between what I call magical and mythic consciousness. People at the "red" level of consciousness, which is also shared by street gangs, warlords, the Mafia, drug lords, soldiers of fortune, guerilla warriors, skinheads, white supremacists, Wild West cowboys, and so forth, are moving beyond the rigidities of tribal magic into a somewhat individualized state where the theme might be "No one tells me what to do." They have not yet been converted to the higher-level religious values of blue mythicism. They may claim, like the Taliban, to be devout Muslims (or Christians). But they are really thugs, members of a gang who glory in violent achievement, individual daring, extreme acting out, and peer approval.

The difference between green consciousness and red consciousness, therefore, is huge. If there is a red street gang selling drugs and occasionally shooting members of rival gangs, we can understand where they are in terms of consciousness development. They—tattoos and all—are at "red." We should have compassion for them and their problems. But when they act out their rage or sell crack cocaine on the street in the presence of children, it is necessary to call the police. So too must be the fate of the Talibans and Al Qaedas of this world.

Green-level consciousness needs to learn this lesson: There are natural hierarchies of consciousness, each with its own worldview and value system; higher levels are far more inclusive and evolved than lower levels; and, in an interdependent world, when people from lower levels act out in an antisocial manner, they need to be stopped.

Another mistaken notion of many with green consciousness is that anything nonrational is postrational. This is seen most clearly in the idealization of ancient tribal and even earlier human societies. For example, many feminists point to a so-called golden age prior to patriarchy when humans worshipped the Goddess. That sometimes thousands upon thousands of humans were routinely sacrificed in many of these cultures is not given much emphasis. Nor are the brutality and shortness of life in those cultures nor the profound limitations of earlier human consciousness compared with that of today. There is much of this mistaken romanticism in the New Age spiritual movement.

Wilber, like many others, also criticizes green consciousness for its cult of the victim. At times it seems as though everyone is a victim in our society. There are now even "victims groups," people whose whole identities are defined by the fact that they were victims of sexual abuse, drunk drivers, terrorists, and even of UFO abductions.

At universities, free speech is curtailed lest people be victimized by having their feelings hurt or their self-esteem wounded. Oppressors are evil. Victims, on the other hand, are morally superior, even entitled to reparations. So, naturally, everyone wants to be a victim. All this, as Wilber points out, is an extreme form of narcissism and, when translated into public policy, can be a creeping form of totalitarianism whereby the thoughts and speech of others, if they are the least bit bothersome, are controlled by law.

At the higher levels of consciousness, one realizes that there are no victims, that all of life is ruled by divine law, and that, if anything, God/the universe is more merciful than just in the troubles it allows to come upon us. Those realizations, however, are beyond the level of realization of the greens.

Even though they emphasize sensitivity to others, it would be a mistake to think that all those with green consciousness have love and compassion for all. They often have love and compassion only for those who agree with them or for those they label as victims. They often despise rednecks, Christian evangelicals, NASCAR races, hunting, professional wrestling, and rap. They are often pleased when blue institutions such as the ministry of a TV evangelist, the Boy Scouts, or the Catholic Church are scandalized and exposed.[4]

Still another "disease" of the emerging green consciousness is essentialism, the idea that only blacks can speak to the black experience, only women for women, only Native Americans for Native Americans. The emphasis is on group rights rather than individual rights, especially the rights of victimized groups. For this reason, for example, conventions of the Democratic Party have quotas for a dozen different groups. This is pluralism and sensitivity carried to an extreme.

Still another fault of many people with green consciousness is the fear of risk. From the soul's point of view, the principal purpose of our life here on Earth, if not the only purpose, is to grow spiritually, that is, to grow in *awareness by experience,* even if that experience is "risky." This, however, is not the goal of most greens. Because many greens do not believe in the soul or the soul's immortality, their goal is simply to live as long and as well as possible—seen in materialistic and physical terms, not in terms of inner spiritual growth. Because their main reason for living, unlike previous generations, is simply to live as long as possible, they hate risks of any sort.

As the Baby Boom generation has aged, the media increasingly reflects this fear-of-risk mentality. Every Fourth of July we are warned of the risks of firecrackers and of *E. coli* bacteria from improperly barbecued hamburgers. Hurricanes are now tracked even as they leave the coast of Africa thousands of miles away. Every Halloween we are warned of poisoned candy and apples with razor blades. Every Christmas we are warned about flammable toys and toys with parts that can be swallowed by small children. Every New Year's and Saint Patrick's Day come the warnings about drunk drivers. Every Memorial Day, as we venture outdoors, we are warned about skin cancer from the ultraviolet rays of the sun, about West Nile disease from mosquitoes, and Lyme disease from ticks.

Public service announcements, paid for with our own taxpayer dollars, are constantly warning us about cigarettes, marijuana, cocaine, breast cancer, colon cancer, the dangers of not wearing seat belts or bicycle helmets, faulty child cribs, improperly installed car seats, alcohol, anthrax, tornadoes, lightning, "unsafe" sex, obesity, fatty foods, cholesterol, terrorists, and on and on and on. Going on an airplane trip has become one of the most unpleasant experiences of contemporary life, with grandmothers told to remove their shoes being only one of all sorts of anti-risk measures now in place (at the cost of billions of dollars).

Every one of these messages, broadcast constantly day and night, introduces fear into our conscious and subconscious minds and, of course, fear *attracts* what is feared. Are we safer now? No. Being in constant fear, we are in far worse danger. But green consciousness has not evolved enough to see the metaphysical truth I just set forth. Greens mistakenly *think* they are safer because of all the fear-mongering.

Green consciousness, though more inner-directed than any of the previous levels, is also still dependent upon "group-think." Greens tend to move in groups and think and vote and have lifestyles like their fellow greens. Their values—as typified by supporting Ben and Jerry's ice cream, voting Democratic, participating in an AIDS walk—are still more cultural than spiritual. Like those at orange (the rational level of conscious-ness) and blue (the later mythic level), they still seek to impose their values upon others through the political process (though their values are more expansive, tolerant, and nuanced). They see themselves in a constant battle with the worldviews of orange and blue. For this and the reasons just given, green is not at peace. It feels as besieged as orange and blue.

Finally, green consciousness, like all those which have pre-ceded it, is convinced that its view of the world is the only legit-imate and true view of the world. Green members of the Democratic Party, therefore, can be every bit as rabid as mythic level (blue) Republicans in fighting the "culture war" that has been ripping America apart for at least ten years now. The polarities, incivility, and gridlock in Congress are the direct products of this war.

While the mythic-level blues and vision-logic greens are fighting, however, the so-called "center" of both Republican and Democratic parties is held firmly by orange, the rational level. That is why both parties, however ideological their blue and green core memberships, are beholden to corporate interests most of all. After all, the campaign money for both parties comes primarily from corporations and large financial institutions.[5] From corporations and their lobbyists also originate many if not most government policies. The political center is the competi-tive, winners and losers, capitalistic, militaristic, patriarchal, exploitative, anti-environmental, commercialistic, rational level.

Even the rise of green has so far not been able to displace rational consciousness as the most powerful consciousness operating in the political arena. Part of the reason is green's own limitations. What then is beyond green? Can we look there for salvation? Let us now explore that possibility.

9
Yellow and Turquoise Consciousness

Psychologists Christopher C. Cowan and Don Edward Beck call all the levels of consciousness up to green the "first tier" of human consciousness. The next two levels (and those above them) are called "second tier." The most important difference is that, while all the levels up to and including green are very egotistic in the sense that people at those levels think their way of seeing the world and their values are the only correct ones, those at the second tier, for the first time, can actually see the whole spiral of consciousness development and can appreciate the contributions made by each level of consciousness. As such, yellow is the first truly integral level.

Yellow and turquoise persons can operate at any of the levels described so far—depending on what is appropriate to the situation. Yellow and turquoise, like green, are sublevels of vision-logic consciousness (though turquoise begins to fade into psychic consciousness, the next higher level). So, for the sake of convenience, I cover both at once. I also cover them together because the number of people at these levels is very low—only a small percentage of the adult American and Western population—though I agree with Wilber that more and more greens will pass into the yellow and turquoise levels in the coming years.

People at both the yellow and turquoise levels are finally becoming inner-directed. They march to their own inner drummers. They are also integrating body, emotions, and mind, the conscious and unconscious aspects of themselves, and so liberating themselves from many of the emotional blockages and debilitating fears that weigh down people at the lower levels. They have also liberated themselves from rigid ideologies and belief systems of all kinds and they begin to appreciate all the wonderful nuances of life, its great complexity, and the contributions of all people—even those with whom one disagrees.

People at yellow and turquoise begin to "go with the flow," letting go of rigid expectations that things or people be a certain way. They are able to roll with the punches and to take things a day at a time. They realize that change is the rule of life here in space-time and they accept that. They stop obsessing about risks and risk factors. They increasingly realize that the more they know and learn the more they don't know—and that the same is true of the medical and other sciences—and they become more and more comfortable living with that uncertainty. They begin to trust life itself rather than a mythic God in the sky, their personal achievements or rank in society, or even the purity of their own good intentions.

People at yellow or turquoise tend to be able to get along with people on all the lower levels because they can "see" where these other people are coming from and act accordingly. As their own egos have shrunk, they tend not to get into partisan bickering of any kind. They like integrated and open systems. They love to solve complex problems and care very little whether they get the credit or not. It is solving the problems that energizes them. They are able to intervene to heal people and systems at all lower levels of the spiral and intuitively know how to move the people up along the spiral to the next level. They aim for win-win solutions for people at all levels.

Yellow and turquoise people learn from anybody at any level. They understand that all people have gifts and talents that can be of service to all. They do not like to waste time, to overconsume, or to create clutter and baggage. They think in the long term, working for the good of future humanity. They accept the ups and downs of life as normal. They will do what they like no matter whether it's popular, trendy, "in," or "out."

Turquoise, as the color implies, moves in more of an overtly spiritual direction than yellow (yellow can be perfectly happy in a fully secular arena). People at the turquoise level begin to see the *inner* connections between all things and people and to more deeply appreciate and value their own interior lives. At turquoise, for the first time, one may actually "see" the whole of creation as a single living organism, a self-creative organism as we described earlier. All of life is seen as imbued with a deep spiritual significance, with transcendent meaning, and with great importance. Turquoise senses the subtle flows that go on within any relationship, family, organization, or society. Turquoise also senses intuitively the natural hierarchies of the great chains of being and consciousness.

People of this color strive to cooperate with that flow and to maximize abundance, both material and spiritual, for all beings. Not that they pile up fortunes. No, they tend to live simply but with great everyday creativity. It is to yellow and turquoise people—with their wonderful integrative abilities— that the planet will have to look for guidance in the twenty-first century. The problems we now face are incapable of being solved by people at any of the first-tier levels of consciousness. None of them see enough, their focus is too narrow, and all of them are at war with each other imagining they are the "one true way." If the human race is to solve its present problems, we must look to people at the yellow and turquoise levels and to those few souls who progress beyond even those levels.

10
The Subtle Realms

In *Putting on the Mind of Christ* I wrote extensively about the next two levels of consciousness, the psychic level and the subtle level, together constituting what I call in this chapter "the subtle realm." Here I offer a brief summary of these levels.

The psychic level is essentially characterized by an identification of the "self" with the "inner witness," no longer with the mind. While many at the psychic level begin to open to intuitive information from beyond the five senses as occurs in clairvoyance (what people normally refer to as "psychic"), that is not the central characteristic of the psychic level. What is more important is that people at the psychic level have definitively "turned within." What is happening inside them, especially their own inner growth in awareness, has become far more important than what is happening in their external world.

They have become spiritual seekers after the meaning of life or seeking union with "God," whom they may define in a number of ways (or, if Buddhist, not mention at all).[1]

Very often people at the psychic level are moved to become meditators and take up a disciplined spiritual path. For they finally "get it," that is, that God is within them and not in the sky somewhere or even in church. The person at the psychic level sees that he has thoughts, but his "I" is not thought or mind. She has emotions, but her "I" is not emotion. He has a body, but his "I" is not the body. One's "I" is now the silent inner witness that witnesses one's thoughts, emotions, and body. In meditation one dives into that "I."

At the psychic level one becomes even more inner-directed than at yellow or turquoise. Ralph Waldo Emerson and Henry David Thoreau are examples of the psychic level and its faith in the self. One also feels a new connection with Nature, a sort of unity with all of nature of the type described by poets such as Wordsworth and Ruskin.

At the subtle level of consciousness, the next level up from the psychic, one opens to all sorts of extremely subtle and creative spiritual energies. Each person's experience will be different because, by the time the soul grows into the subtle level, it has become greatly individuated, having integrated all the experiences of many lifetimes, often liberating those experiences from the depths of the unconscious. The wisdom gained in these experiences is collected and kept. The pain and suffering of all those experiences are gradually released, thus purifying the soul and the body to go to higher vibrational levels.

The subtle level, at which all one's gross neuroses and selfish attitudes have been healed, is generally a level of great creative activity. There is inner freedom from all the stultifying dogmas and practices of organized religion, yet at a deeper level there is a deeper understanding of the spiritual truths buried under all the dogma, rituals, moralisms, and practices.

Wilber describes the subtle level as the level of "saints," people who have labored mightily to serve and spiritualize and illumine the human race.[2] It is generally hard to label historical characters, especially if they have not written detailed spiritual autobiographies, but to name only Americans, examples might be Clara Barton, Booker T. Washington, George Washington Carver, Emily Dickinson, Walt Whitman, Albert Einstein,[3] Martin Luther King Jr., Abraham Lincoln, Elizabeth Ann Seton, Katherine Drexel, Ernest Holmes, and Edgar Cayce.[4] All of these individuals dedicated their lives in one way or another to the uplifting of the human spirit.

At the subtle level, relatively speaking, there is very little ego left. So people like those listed have performed their services for humanity with little concern for adulation or compensation from others. If there is a fault at the subtle level, it is that persons at that level sometimes tend to be crusaders out to change the world. Because they still identify their "I" with their human personalities, they may sometimes rely too much on their own force of personality to change things and other people, rather than letting go of expectations and relying on Spirit to accomplish the work through them. But they are great souls, each and every one. The future of humanity depends upon many more people attaining this level of consciousness, caring, and creativity.

One of the principal features of the subtle realm (the psychic and subtle levels of consciousness) is constant realization. As people pass through these levels of consciousness, they are continually amazed at the new insights into truth that they are given as vast new inner worlds open before the inner eye. With Christians (and I imagine it's the same with Buddhists, Muslims, and Hindus with respect to their own scriptures) these new realizations are especially noticeable with respect to the Bible, particularly the New Testament, and even more particularly with the words of Jesus. One may have read or heard the same scripture passage a thousand times before but, all of a sudden, it has a fresh meaning, a deeper meaning, yields an unexpected new understanding, even offers a revelation. Teresa of Avila called these new insights "intellectual visions."

These intellectual visions, like all else about the spiritual life, are also evolving. What would have been a great revelation in a prior age (for example, the revelation of the Pythagorean theorem to the spiritual master Pythagoras in ancient Greece) is now taught in middle schools in contemporary America. What is true for mathematical, artistic, and scientific advancements is also true of spiritual revelations. Just as 90 percent of the world's greatest scientists of all time are alive today, so too, as Wilber posits, the world's greatest mystics and spiritual adepts are probably also alive today.

It is not that these contemporary souls are any holier or closer to God than those of the past. It is just that the human race has evolved. It is capable of much clearer understandings now than in the days when Jesus had to cloak his truths in parables. Things can now be spelled out in clear language rather than remain hidden in mythology and symbolism. Furthermore, new implications of scriptural truths can be unfolded in ourselves and society. The abolition of slavery, for example, was a new and terribly important unfolding of the implications of Jesus' teachings in the nineteenth century, as was the movement for the equality of women in the twentieth century. Revelations continue. It is true, in one sense, that the whole of the Christian revelation is contained in Jesus Christ, but that does not mean that the depth of what Jesus taught or the full implications thereof are anywhere near being completely unfolded yet.

It is to be expected that as a person passes through the subtle realms (or even taps into those realms in meditation) new insights into spiritual truth will come to that person. Such people have now grown enough in maturity and spiritual depth to be entrusted with the role of teachers and are provided with the material to be taught.

Sri Yukteswarji Giri, the guru of the famous Indian/American yogi Paramahansa Yogananda (author of *Autobiography of a Yogi*), was once visited by a teacher of Hindu theology. The man expounded on the Bhagavad Gita, which is perhaps the most important revealed Hindu scripture.[5] The man spoke on and on about this interpretation and that interpretation and what scholars x, y, and z had said about a scriptural passage. Sri Yukteswarji was unsatisfied and kept asking the man, "But what is *your* insight into the meaning of the passage?" Finally, the theologian had to admit that he understood the Gita only at an intellectual level and had no personal inner realizations.

Sri Yukteswarji had made his point. Inner realization with respect to any scripture, including the Bible, comes only with deep meditation and growth in personal holiness. The scriptures—for example, the Gospel of John—are written at the causal level of consciousness, the Christ Consciousness. When "Jesus" speaks in the Gospel of John, it is not Jesus of Nazareth speaking, but the eternal Christ. Scripture, therefore, cannot be correctly understood at the rational level, let alone a lower level such as the mythic, no matter how many Bible study classes one attends or theology courses one takes.

One of the revelations I received when I passed through the subtle level was that "we will everything that happens to us beforehand." Those were the words that came to me when I finally "saw" with my inner eye that I myself had created everything that had been happening in my life. This was such a startling revelation to me that I thought I might be deluded. So I called a woman contemplative who was then a mentor to me and asked her if it was true.

She assured me that not only was it true, but it was commonplace for contemplatives and mystics (contemplatives with some psychic abilities) to make this discovery when going through the subtle realm. Afterwards I learned that "we create our own reality" is a staple of New Age belief and that the belief has been in the popular religious culture in America ever since the beginning of the "New Thought" movement (see the following discussion). However, because this belief is often misunderstood and misinterpreted, some historical background may be helpful.

Protestant reformers such as Martin Luther and John Calvin (and counter-reformers such as Ignatius of Loyola) were in the forefront of trying to educate and initiate the Christian masses to move from the mythic into the rational level of consciousness, particularly through the dissemination of the written scriptures to the general public. But, by and large, the early Protestant reformers did not tamper with the essentially mythic content of the Christian Creed. By the early nineteenth century in America, however, a new group of religious thinkers had arisen who began to "rationalize" (make "scientific") some of the deeper meanings of the Christian scriptures.

The grandfather of this "New Thought" movement was the mystic Phineas Quimby (1802–1866), a "mental healer" who set up practice in Maine. Quimby taught that there was no error, disease, or even death in the mind of God, that God was immanent in humans, that indeed our minds were a part of God's mind, and that error, disease, and even death were caused by our false mental beliefs. The whole of the universe, taught Quimby, was pervaded by divine intelligence, and the physical world of matter continually arises out of that intelligence. If we could attune ourselves to the inner mind of God like Jesus did, we could free ourselves from error, disease, and even death.

As often happens with spiritual teachers, Quimby's chief disciples came to him for healing in the years shortly before his death in 1866. One, Warren Felt Evans (1817–1889) later wrote extensively, including the books *Esoteric Christianity and Mental Therapeutics* and *Mental Cure*. Two others, Julius Dresser (1838–1893) and his wife, Annetta Seabury, were apparently the first to use the "New Thought" label and wrote a great deal about conquering disease with the mind. Finally, the most famous of all was Mary Baker Eddy, who in 1875 published her *Science and Health: With Key to the Scriptures* and founded Christian Science.

Eddy certainly had her faults. Grave faults. She was autocratic, ego-inflated, neurotic, and uneducated in philosophy, theology, and psychology. The religion she founded, Christian Science, was in large part a personality cult that considered her every word and action divine and infallible, and which she used to enrich her own worldly power, wealth, and fame. She so much emphasized "mind over matter" (to her, "matter" was nonexistent and/or evil) that she discouraged the use of exoteric medicine, with the result that countless followers—men, women, and children—were consigned to grave suffering and even death in the avoidance of medical assistance.

Despite these serious limitations, Eddy's genius in setting forth the mental basis for the miracles of the Gospels was a distinctly new revelation in the sense in which I describe revelation in this chapter. She taught, for example, that Jesus did not so much "raise" Lazarus from the dead as refuse to accept the belief that Lazarus was dead in the first place. Jesus insisted—that is, held to this belief with absolute undoubting faith—that Lazarus was not dead, but sleeping, and so he called him forth from the tomb. Likewise, Jesus, making use of the faith of those he healed, held to the inner belief of their "perfect health" no matter what external appearances to the contrary and no matter the beliefs of the confused crowds. Thus Eddy, along with Quimby, Evans, and the Dressers, introduced to the world a rational, scientific approach to the miracles of the Gospels.

Many others followed them. Emma Curtis Hopkins (1853–1925), a sometime disciple of Eddy, wrote *Scientific Christian Mental Practice*. Hopkins, in turn, taught Charles (1854–1948) and Myrtle (1845–1931) Fillmore, who founded the Unity School of Christianity (which now has hundreds of member churches). Charles Fillmore wrote *Jesus Christ Heals, Christian Healing, Prosperity, Teach Us to Pray*, and many other influential books. Another of Hopkins' students was Ernest Holmes (1887–1960), who founded the Religious Science/ Science of Mind movement (which also numbers hundreds of churches) and whose 1926 book *The Science of Mind* is still in print.

Eventually, the ideas of the New Thought movement influenced the contemporary New Age movement and even mainstream Christianity, for example, Rev. Dr. Norman Vincent Peale's 1950s bestseller *The Power of Positive Thinking*. Unfortunately, some of the teachings have been corrupted in the sense that their deeper meanings are not understood by people at lower levels of consciousness. I have been to a Science of Mind church where many use positive mental affirmations solely for materialistic reasons, for example, to manifest a new Lexus.

This materialistic approach also seems to be gaining ground with the preachers of the "gospel of prosperity," which is peddled to many poor people in America and Brazil. Often only the preachers end up with the riches. It is also the basis of self-help and get-ahead-of-others doctrines preached by many self-help and success-oriented secular teachers. This is not putting on the mind of Christ or aligning oneself, in surrender, to the soul. It is spirituality in the service of the ego.

Another area of error was introduced by Eddy herself. Eddy did not know about the various levels of consciousness, so she expected ordinary believers, people at the mythic or rational level, to have the same kind of faith, belief, mental discipline, and single-minded power of manifestation that Jesus had. That is why she discouraged the use of physicians. But most people do not have anywhere near the faith required to routinely heal themselves. Nor have they grown enough spiritually to manifest things powerfully, as Jesus did.

Such ability to cure diseases (and to manifest prosperity as in the multiplying of the loaves and fishes) takes great vibrational power of the type encountered only in the higher levels of consciousness, and for good reason. Only people who are very spiritual and selfless and have a great sense of responsibility can be entrusted by the universe with such powers. People at a lesser level of awareness would create damage and problems with such powers. It was a mistake, therefore, for Eddy to teach people to avoid doctors—a teaching that has too often had disastrous results.

The teachings of Quimby and Eddy, like most of religion in the nineteenth century, tended to denigrate the body. Quimby and Eddy, in fact, tended to an extreme idealism in which matter and the body were seen as illusion. Matter and the body, however, even though they do arise out of the spiritual realm, are not illusions here in space-time, and their province must be respected. You can throw yourself off a building (as Satan tempted Jesus) using any positive mental affirmations you like, but you will still fall to the ground and be killed. Eventually, as the scriptures predict, we may be able to eat poison or handle venomous snakes without being hurt—but it would be foolhardy for the average believer to attempt this.[6]

We grow spiritually *in the body* as the yogis have known for centuries (and as the Ascension of Jesus in the body mythically signifies). We cannot neglect the body, overruling it with the mind. Doing so during the Age of Reason has caused immense damage to Western psyches. The body must be honored and listened to, not overridden, if we are to grow spiritually into the highest levels of consciousness.

Finally, it is important, when entertaining beliefs such as "I mentally create my own reality," to distinguish what "mind" is being referenced. We have at least three minds. First, we have our everyday conscious mind, which operates at the rational level and which chatters away all the time entertaining both positive and negative thoughts. This is the "mind" that New Thought seeks to discipline through positive mental affirmations and other techniques. There is nothing wrong with this. It is an important step forward in spiritual understanding. After all, Jesus taught that we are responsible for every one of our thoughts. But, like their nineteenth- and early-twentieth-century contemporaries, the teachers of New Thought were heavily influenced by rationalism, the rational level of consciousness that was then supreme in the West. So they tended to overemphasize the importance of the everyday rational mind.

Second, we have a subconscious mind that is programmed by both positive and negative beliefs. New Thought also attempts to reprogram that mind by releasing negative false beliefs and substituting positive beliefs. This is a useful and important spiritual discipline, but it does nothing about the emotions. I have seen people in New Thought churches making positive affirmations until they are blue in the face but, because many of the people have severe emotional damage, they do not succeed in healing their diseases or manifesting in their lives what they need. The emotions operate according to their own laws and cannot be healed with the mind (though insight into the causes of emotional problems is often very helpful). Other techniques, such as meditation and emotional release, must be employed to free up our emotions so we can move on to the next level.

Third, we have the "Mind of Christ," the mind of the soul that operates at the Christ or causal consciousness level. Though he wrote no books, it seems to me that this is the "mind" to which the mystic Quimby was referring (as were other great New Thought teachers such as Emma Curtis Hopkins, Ernest Holmes, and Charles Fillmore). This "mind" includes the everyday mind, the subconscious mind, the emotions, and the Christ Mind—but with the accent on aligning ourselves with the last.

When I had the revelation that "I will everything that happens to me beforehand," I was already four years into the Dark Night of the Soul, the juncture in the spiritual life where one's identification of one's "I" with the personality (including the everyday and subconscious minds) is disintegrating (see *Putting on the Mind of Christ*). When I had that revelation, therefore, I was beginning to "see" with the Mind of Christ, with spiritual eyes, and from the point of view of the soul. It was the soul, therefore, that had willed everything beforehand, not the personality.

The Mind of Christ is not so much a "mind" as a particular level of consciousness, the Christ Consciousness. When we get to that level, God willing, we will be able to see panoramically, realizing, among other things, that all things work together for the good, that all is perfect, and that all is in divine order—even sickness. We will no longer use spirituality in the service of ego needs but, trusting that all else will be added, we will spend ourselves entirely in the service of others, never worrying about what we will eat or put on. We will stop all our efforts to manifest health or anything else *knowing* that, in Christ, we already possess all of these things and more.

What I am emphasizing in this chapter and in all of part 2 is that, with the outside mythic God now dead, we will increasingly have to rely upon the unfoldment of the God within ourselves, the realization of our own divinity. This unfoldment takes place in stages that have been mapped by contemplatives and mystics throughout the ages. With this unfoldment come new realizations, new spiritual powers, and new levels of responsibility. Evolved souls are normally expected by the universe to accomplish great things. They are also expected to use their new or enhanced powers wisely, lovingly, and in the service of others.

This chapter and the ones to follow are intended to briefly describe the higher levels of consciousness and some of the realizations and spiritual powers that one can expect to encounter at those levels. I have just described realizations and powers with respect to healing. Now I turn to the realizations and powers involved in manifesting in space-time exactly what one needs.

11
Lessons of the Subtle Realm—
Manifesting What One Needs

In the previous chapter, I touched upon manifesting what one needs in the context of healing. In this chapter, I want to cover the same subject in a broader sense. Manifestation may sound mysterious and sometimes is so (how did Jesus multiply loaves and raise the dead?), but it is something all of us have been doing all our lives. Do we have a place to live? If so, we have manifested it. Do we have enough to eat? If so, we have manifested it. Do we own a motor vehicle? If so, we have manifested it. Do we have a spouse or partner? If so, we have manifested him or her. Do we have a job? If so, we have manifested it. Are there negative things in our lives? If so, we—at least at the soul level—have manifested them too. Manifestation is something we do constantly, but most of the time we do it unconsciously, not even knowing how we produce these daily miracles.

What one often learns when one's consciousness enters the subtle realm (the psychic/subtle level of consciousness) is how to manifest *consciously*. Think back over the principal things you manifested in your life, for example, your spouse or your career. What went into making your career happen? How did you do it? How was it that you were in the right place at the right time and made connections with the right people? With respect to your spouse, how did you meet him or her? What were the circumstances? Who introduced you? Think of the timing and all the so-called coincidences that might have been involved.

Many people have wondrous stories to tell about how they met and connected with their spouses and about how they found their life's careers. These stories are wondrous, magical, even miraculous. That was manifestation—big time—in our lives and, if we examine the process carefully, we can learn many lessons from these life events.

When I graduated from law school, I had the usual round of interviews with big law firms that sent representatives to my school to interview students. But I didn't want to work for a big law firm. I also explored jobs in city government, with small law firms, and at the state government level, but I didn't want those either. What I wanted was a job with the federal government in Washington where I could be of public service at a high level. But I had no connections. Nor did I have the time or money to go to Washington for interviews. My desire, however, was strong and clear: I wanted what I called a first-class job in Washington with the federal government and I trusted that God would so provide.

In February of my last year of law school, my father was sent on a business trip to Washington, D.C., and decided to drive and take my mother. They let me come along. I readied a pile of resumes and off we went. We had one day in Washington. As I said, I had no connections and no interviews set up. All I had were the resumes and about six hours to get them out. So I took cabs from one federal agency to another and dropped the resumes in the human resources departments. That was all I had time to do. Maybe six agencies in all, one being the Department of Labor. Then I let it all go, got back in the car, and went home for the rest of the school year.

A couple of months after we returned home to New England, my father happened to mention my job hunt to a friend of his at work. This friend had a friend who was a lawyer with the Labor Department in Washington. We were all Boston Irish Catholics, and the man in Washington worked in an office headed by another Irish Catholic. As a result, I got my only interview in June, was immediately hired, and began an extremely interesting, well-paying, emotionally satisfying job where I advanced to a high-grade level and then to a political position in the Carter administration within five years. I was able to buy a house on Capitol Hill and made a huge number of very dear friends, all of whom are friends to this day.

This is classic manifestation and, like all true manifestation, it defies all the odds and proves (to those who take the time to notice) that the universe is not run by chance but by divine law in which we ourselves are operative participators.

Gregg Braden gives an excellent example of manifestation in his book *The Isaiah Effect: Decoding the Lost Science of Prayer and Prophecy*. Braden recounts how, in the third year of a drought in the American Southwest, he accompanied a Native American named David into the desert "to call to the rain." "Today," David said, "we pray rain."[1] After David spent a few minutes walking around with his eyes closed, he got ready to leave. Braden, surprised, asked, "Already? I thought you were going to pray for rain." "No," David replied, "I said I would 'pray rain.' If I had prayed *for* rain, it could never happen."[2]

(Emphasis in original.) That afternoon it rained—so much that there were road washouts and flash floods.

David avoided the mistake that most of us make when we pray. In praying *for* something, what we are actually doing is declaring to God (the sole power underlying the laws of the universe) that we *lack* whatever it is we want. We are saying, in effect, I *lack* rain. God hears and *accepts* that affirmation of lack by us, the cocreators of the universe, and makes the lack come true. No rain comes. No healing comes. No money comes. We have *created* lack versus abundance.

Instead, as David explained to Braden, we must visualize what we want and "see" it coming into our lives. No doubts. Feel the rain, feel the healing, feel the green dollar bills in our hands and overflowing our pockets. Then, as Jesus taught us, we thank God ahead of time for making what we want come to pass, for, as Jesus said, God already knew our needs. God was merely waiting for us to take our own power as cocreators and create our own abundance using the proper method of manifestational prayer. David explained, "Creation is already complete. Our prayer becomes a prayer of thanks for the *opportunity* to choose which creation we experience. Through our thanks, we honor all possibilities and bring the ones we choose into this world."[3] (Emphasis in original.)

The best book on manifestation I have ever read is called *The Laws of Manifestation*. It is by David Spangler, who has written several brilliant books on the subject, all of which, unfortunately, are out of print. So I will try to teach what Spangler taught me by paraphrasing him in my own words. When one manifests, one is not doing magic but "translating" energy either up or down, from one level to another. When an author writes a book, he translates mental energy into a physical form. An artist can translate emotional energy into a physical painting. A politician can use mental energy to create emotional energy in a crowd.

Spangler notes that manifestation is not creating something out of nothing but rather is making visible or "manifest" that which already exists in an invisible state. "Heat was potential in the coal," he writes. "Health is potential within illness. Abundance is potential within poverty. Divinity is potential within humanity."[4] Just as God manifested through the power of his word—"Let there be light"—so we, too, manifest especially by our speech. If we say things such as "I can never do anything right," it will become a self-fulfilling prophecy (and so will a similar subconscious belief put there by a parent long ago).

It is crucial, therefore, to always make positive affirmations. Spangler writes, "The clue to manifestation lies in the recognition that God in His Wholeness is the only reality. Everything in the universe is directly or indirectly related to everything else through this Wholeness and there is no barrier or impediment of time, space, or circumstance that can obstruct the right flow of energy between affinities within the Whole."[5]

There are four levels of manifestation: physical, emotional, mental, and soul. We manifest physically when we work for a living. We manifest emotionally when we put our heart and soul into some project while trusting that God will bring it success. (At the emotional level, worry can sabotage even the heart's desire.) We manifest mentally when we visualize what we want and make positive affirmation, not of "wanting" or "lacking," but of already possessing. Finally, we manifest at the soul level by realizing that we are not mere human personalities. We are the Christ, the Word from which the entire universe is born. Therefore, we already possess all things, having been given them by the Father from all eternity.

The entire universe already exists within us. When we manifest, we are simply God expressing divine creativity. We manifest for the same reason that God manifests, namely, for the sheer pleasure and enjoyment and creativity of it, not because we "need" anything. As David Spangler writes, "The need and interest of soul consciousness is not how to draw things to itself from the environment but how to draw out from itself the qualities and energies from which a greater environment can emerge."[6]

From the personality's viewpoint, abundance is a quantity. Abundance means more, more, and more. But from the soul's viewpoint, abundance is a quality, a being at oneness with the inner essence of all things. The soul nevertheless still uses the lesser vehicles of body, emotions, and mind in exercising its divine creativity. It still works hard, desires keenly, and thinks clearly. One cannot win the lottery without getting a ticket. The necessary work must be done.

An important part of manifestation is giving thanks, even before the desired result occurs. This completes the cycle of energy. It is also important to release back into the universe all that which no longer serves. Many people are unable to manifest new things, new ideas, or even spiritual growth into their lives because they are holding onto tons of old stuff (physical, emotional, mental) they no longer need or use.

Spangler teaches that soul-level manifestation requires right identification, right imagination, right attunement, and right action. Right identification requires identifying not with our space-time personalities, but with our Higher Self. From the viewpoint of the Higher Self, there is no lack, for we already contain all things. We need only *express* them for the glory of God (not for ego purposes). Right imagination requires meditating on how, what, and why we want to manifest. It requires us to see that all potential lies within ourselves and that the essence of exactly what we need can be formed there. It requires us to determine what our souls desire, which may or may not be what our personalities desire.

Right attunement means cloaking the spiritual essence of

the desired manifestation in mental (visualization), emotional (energetic), and physical form so that it becomes present to us in space-time. Right action requires that we do the space-time work that is necessary to bring about the result, which includes letting go of old baggage to make way for the new.

Once we have put it out to the universe, we must then let go, trusting God to bring us what we need, never doubting, never entertaining any negativity or worries, just fiercely "holding to" the *knowing* that the desired manifestation will indeed manifest. If we can do this, the result is foolproof.

Manifestation at the soul level as I have just described it is not easy, however, for to be done properly it requires that one's consciousness be at the soul level, the causal or Christ Consciousness level. To pray "in Jesus' name" means that we must have put on the Mind of Christ ourselves. That is possible only when we move beyond the subtle levels of consciousness into the Christ or causal level, and that requires the ego to die ("unless the seed dies"). By this I mean we must realize that "we" are not our personalities. "We" in fact do not exist. Only God exists. God is the only power.

We, like all else of Creation, are merely avenues for God's expression, means by which God operates in this world. To consciously manifest, therefore, is to consciously participate in God's own creative action, bringing forth in love and beauty that which will serve ourselves and others. Manifestation is a sacred trust, for we are using the powers of God, the God in whom we live and move and *have our being*. It is all God, and at the next level, the causal, one will realize that once and for all.

12
Lessons of the Subtle Realm–
Understanding the Law of Karma

In *Putting on the Mind of Christ* I explained that Jesus, Saint Paul, and even the Old Testament taught what Buddhists and Hindus call the law of karma. Christians do not have a name for karma, but it could be called "the spiritual law of cause and effect." "He who lives by the sword shall die by the sword," said Jesus (Matt. 26:52). "A man will reap what he sows," taught Saint Paul (Gal. 6:7–8). "An eye for an eye and a tooth for a tooth," explained the Old Testament (Lev. 24:20; Deut. 19:21). That is why Jesus admonished, "Do unto others what you wish to have done to you" (Matt. 7:12).

A Catholic woman who had read *Putting on the Mind of Christ* wrote to me to, among other things, object to my acceptance of the law of karma. Like many other Christians, she apparently interprets karma as meaning "sin." She wrote to me that "Sin is the loss of eternal life with God . . . The Redeemer [Jesus, understood as a "god" who "came down from" heaven and incarnated as a human] puts an end to the belief in a universal law of karma . . . because he pays our debts and restores what was lost . . . either Christ paid all karmic debt or he didn't." She wrote further that "a more hideous view cannot be imagined" than the "view of innocent babes being paid back for bad karma in a previous life."

This reader expresses the confusion of many when it comes to this subject. So I will try to explain karma more clearly. First, contrary to the reader's view and as I set out above, Jesus *taught* the law of karma. He did not "abolish" it any more than he did the law of gravity. Second, karma, which can be positive, negative, or neutral, is not "sin" in the theological sense of an offense against God.[1] Karma has nothing to do with "sin." Nor does it have anything to do with "punishment" or being "paid back." Karma is simply an impersonal law like the law of gravity: "What you sow you will reap," as Saint Paul taught. If you step off a 50-story building, you will certainly fall and be killed. It does not matter if you are a saint or a sinner. It is simply the law of gravity at work. The law of karma works with the same impersonality.

What you do unto others will be done unto you. Simple as that.[2] Karma, as spiritual law, is the spiritual equivalent of the physical law expressed by the second law of thermodynamics, that is, "for every action there is an equal and opposite reaction." *Karma,* a Sanskrit word, simply means "action."

The woman found it "hideous" that "innocent" babes might inherit negative karma from a past life. I have several responses: First, it is an assumption that babes are always "innocent." Paramahansa Yogananda tells of the time that he was handed a little baby to be blessed. When he tuned into the energy of the child, he "saw" that the child had been a murderer in a past life and almost instinctively dropped the little darling.

Second, the idea that Jesus died a bloody death on the cross to appease a ghoulish Sky God Father for our sins seems equally "hideous" to many Christians and others today. For example, popular writer and playwright Daniel Curzon, in his essay "Why I Am an Ex-Catholic," writes, "Just look at the following objectively [rationally]: God decided to have his son born of a virgin in an obscure village and then crucified like a common criminal in order to save a bunch of human beings who were born damned—and why? Because they had inherited an Original Sin from two people who had eaten some forbidden fruit after God told them not to . . . If anyone said that a cult in Guyana was teaching innocent children doctrines like this, the government would arrest the whole lot of them, and should."[3]

If Curzon, who had a Catholic education including four years at a Jesuit college, finds the basic Christian myth (which is just as fundamental to Protestantism and Orthodox Christianity as it is to Catholicism) not only incredible—that is, unbelievable—but even ludicrous and abhorrent, what does one suppose the secular rationalist thinks of that myth? To a rapidly increasing number of Christians and non-Christians, the basic Christian myth no longer makes any sense. Like most of the West for most of the last two thousand years, and the woman who wrote to me, most people once accepted belief in the basic Christian myth as a "given." But that is an assumption that increasingly no longer holds true.

I agree with American Episcopal Bishop John Shelby Spong, author of *Why Christianity Must Change or Die* and *A New Christianity for a New World: Why Traditional Faith Is Dying and How a New Faith Is Being Born,* and with Australian Catholic theologian Michael Morwood, author of *Is Jesus God?* They say that unless Christianity translates the basic Christian myth into understanding, language, and institutional forms that are accessible to, and acceptable to, the postmodern world, Christianity as an institution will die. New wineskins (religious forms) will be produced to hold the new, deeper, and more adequate understandings of Jesus' teachings.

Some Christian denominations such as the Roman Catholic hold to the notion that Jesus' promise that the gates of hell would not prevail against his *ecclesia* (community) apply to their particular Christian sect (even though Jesus had no intention of founding a religion or sect). They do not. They apply to those *who hear the word of God and keep it,* not to any particular human institution.

Some Christian denominations, again including the Roman Catholic, put their hope in the expectation that millions of mythic-level Christians in Latin America and Africa will soon replace the de-Christianized West as the center of the Church.[4] But that is like putting one's bet on the cultures of the Incas and Aztecs to prevail over that of Christopher Columbus and the Spanish conquistadors in 1500 C.E. Those with a lower-level consciousness, one less adequate in coping with today's globalized environment, simply cannot prevail, a lesson fundamentalist Muslims (those few who are prone to violence) are now in the process of learning the hard way.

Mythic Christianity may flourish among the masses in Africa and Latin America for another few generations (a step up from the prior magical level of consciousness), but the educated elites of those nations have in many instances already moved beyond mythic Christianity's limitations. Moreover, the ever-increasing exposure of the masses to the Internet and other forms of global communications will make holding onto a mythic worldview increasingly difficult because the mythic worldview, by definition, is sociocentric—that is, my country, race, religion is the one, true, and only one.

To get back to the Catholic woman reader's assertion about the innocence of newborn infants: As was alluded to by Curzon, Christianity has never viewed babies as "innocent." Under Christian theology, since the earliest days of the Church, babies are born in "original sin." The doctrine of "original sin" (where the word "sin" does not mean any personal fault) is the Christian way of trying to express the truth of negative karmic inheritance. Babies are born "into" the unenlightened condition of the human race. They inherit this darkness and, according to Christian doctrine, babies who die unbaptized cannot enter the kingdom of heaven, Jesus' death on the cross notwithstanding.[5]

This teaching, harsh though it may seem, is correct. It merely spells out the reality of the matter. The "kingdom of heaven" means the Christ Consciousness, enlightenment, and the causal level of consciousness. The consciousness of babies, pursuant to their inheritance as human beings, begins at the archaic/beige level. So, naturally, if they die, they cannot enter heaven.[6] It is not punishment. It is what is. They will have plenty of other lifetimes in which to grow. As the doctrine of the Ascension of Jesus implies, human beings can only enter the kingdom of heaven, the Christ Consciousness, while they are incarnate—which means they at least have to live long enough.

Karma, writes Ken Wilber, is "the inheritance of the past." It is the passing on to us, individually and collectively, of the habits of the past. That is what the doctrine of "original sin" is trying to convey. You may remember that, in an earlier chapter, the philosopher Bruteau noted that evolution in space-time needs two things (two polar opposites) to unfold: stability and novelty. Karma is the stable element. Karma is what we inherit from the past whereas novelty (Wilber uses the word "creativity") is what is newly emerging in the present.

Let me give some examples: If you are born into a middle-class family in the richest country on Earth, the United States, you inherit the collective positive economic karma. If you were born into a slave-owning family two hundred years ago, you would have inherited the negative karma of that family and, spiritually, would have had to overcome that legacy. If you are born as a female in Saudi Arabia, you must contend with that nation's negative karmic habits with respect to women. Likewise, if you are born into a family where a parent (or parents) is a child abuser, you inherit that negative family karma. Child-abusing is a negative karmic habit that may have been going on in that family for centuries for the simple reason that the children of child abusers tend to grow up to become abusers themselves until someone finally grows spiritually and breaks the karmic chain.

We inherit karma on the physical level (our genes), the emotional/psychic level (the habits we carry over from past lives), the soul level (the level of consciousness we realized in past lives), and the cultural level (the family, society, religion, economic status we are born into). That is our inheritance. It can be positive, negative, or neutral.

If you are born into a society that has progressed spiritually only to the tribal/magical/purple level, it will be very difficult to overcome the stability/inertia of that karmic inheritance and to progress to higher levels of consciousness such as the causal or Christ Consciousness. Because of that karmic inheritance, the odds are very heavy against your ever realizing enlightenment in that lifetime. That is why Jesus said that "a man's enemies [spiritually] are members of his own household" and why you have to leave the dead to bury the dead (even your own father), and why he came to set one family member against another.

If anyone is going to hold you back spiritually, you can almost guarantee it will be your own relatives and your own church and culture. They provide cultural stability/inertia—the polar opposite of the novelty/creativity one needs to become an individuated conscious Christ. Of course, if you had realized a high level of consciousness in a prior life, you might quickly recapitulate that level and thus move well beyond your culture—as Jesus himself did, but at what turned out to be a fatal price. People at lower levels of consciousness love their darkness and mightily resist the light. Karmic inertia is very strong at the lower levels for the simple reason that these levels have been habits of human consciousness for many thousands of years.

Karma, therefore, consists of inherited habits—whether the habits be the general level of consciousness of a whole society, the habits of a family, or the individual habits of one's soul. These habits can be positive, negative, or neutral. Thomas Aquinas defined "virtue" as a positive habit and "vice" as a negative habit. Karma consists of positive (virtues), negative (vices), and neutral (blue eyes) inheritances.

Another mistaken notion, perhaps more common in the East than in the West, is that karma is "fate." Someone may be murdered or raped. Some people will conclude, "It must have been their karma." Well, maybe it was and maybe it wasn't. Karma, or the inheritance of the past, is only one side of the evolutionary coin. The other side, which like karma is present in all human situations, is the law of novelty or creativity. No moment or situation is ever exactly like the past. Every situation contains novel, creative elements that have never been seen or experienced before. Otherwise everything about life would be predetermined and predestined and no evolution could occur at all. Everything would be an effect of a past cause. That is not the case.

In fact, the universe is designed in such a way that it "tilts" toward higher and higher levels of complexity—from atoms to molecules to cells to organisms, from lower levels of consciousness to higher levels. In that sense, therefore, the law of novelty and complexity is stronger than the law of karma (lucky for us). In the end, karma is overcome whenever a new level of complexity, awareness, and freedom is realized.

So things are always happening that have never happened before. People make choices unlike those they've made before. People even overcome strong karmic habits such as drug addictions to move into greater personal freedom. Conversely, people may use their free will to commit murder or rape and, while it is true that the soul of the "victim" has to some extent collaborated in these crimes for its own reasons, those reasons may have nothing to do with past karma.

Was Jesus killed because of past karma? Extremely unlikely. But he was killed as an example to us of the seriousness of the death and resurrection that are needed for us to come into Christ Consciousness. Another person may be killed because it was time to leave the Earth and that happened to be the quickest and easiest way to go at the moment. We simply do not know. Or someone may be killed by pure random chance or a deleterious genetic mutation. There are indeed true accidents and randomness—at least as far as the design and operation of space-time is concerned.[7] All these are needed to allow evolution to proceed in the most creative way.

Karma may become very important as we get to the end of the subtle realms and enter into what John of the Cross labeled the "Dark Night of the Soul," the crucifixional passage that ushers us into the causal or Christ Consciousness. In the Dark Night we are baptized with Jesus into his death and then resurrected to a brand new life as Christed beings.[8] In that passage we have to come to grips with, and transform, what John of the Cross calls the "roots" of our sinfulness.

In other words, we encounter *consciously* the deep karmic wounds we inherited from other of our soul's incarnations (whether we inherit this karma directly or by morphic resonance or in some other manner I do not know). The Dark Night of the Soul and the resurrection into what Christian contemplatives have traditionally called the "unitive way" and what Buddhists and Hindus call enlightenment is an extremely radical transformation. We become "new creatures," in the words of Saint Paul.

All along the course of evolution we have seen that lesser wholes (what Wilber and others call holons) combine to make radically new wholes or holons that include the former but radically transcend them and so produce something entirely novel. Hydrogen gas and oxygen, also a gas, combine to give us the wondrous gift of water. The same thing happens during the transformation of the Dark Night of the Soul. A qualitatively new creature is born, no longer *Homo sapiens* but *Homo spiritus*. Just as the lesser transformations were caused by the uniting of holons (whole/parts) into one, I believe this spiritual transformation entails the unification of all our soul's incarnations into one great spirit. That is why we must deal with and transform the negative residues of other lives (while redeeming all their positive qualities and experiences).

We may still look to others as though we are human personalities, but we are not. We are a Christ. We live, now not "we," but Christ lives within us and expresses through us. Jesus, speaking as the Christ, said, "I am the vine and you are the branches." Up until now we have identified with our present or prior personalities, the branches. That is no longer the case. Now all the branches have been unified into one spiritual whole. From now on we, like Jesus, are a vine that bears much fruit. It is to that consciousness that we next turn.

13

Causal Consciousness–Christ Consciousness, the Goal of Evolutionary Spirituality

Causal (and later nondual) consciousness is the goal of the spiritual life (and hence of human evolution on this planet) in both the West and the East. It is the level of consciousness that Jesus called the kingdom of heaven or the kingdom of God and that Hindus and Buddhists call enlightenment. It is the level of consciousness at which we no longer identify with our human personality as our "I" but identify with Christ (Spirit) as our true essence.

At the causal level we can see clearly that we are immortal, that we were never born and will never die and, most important, we can see clearly that we and God are one and that God is the only one who exists. We can also see clearly that we are one with God (and always have been) and are one with all humans (and, indeed, all of Creation). Christians call the causal level the level of Christ Consciousness.

This unity consciousness with God and others is the chief characteristic of causal consciousness. Some Eastern religions call this level of consciousness "enlightenment."

Jesus of Nazareth, who personified and manifested the Christ Consciousness, and who speaks as a personification of the Christ Consciousness in the Gospel of John (i.e., as the Christ), was perhaps the first human being to fully become *Homo spiritus* rather than merely *Homo sapiens*. Walter Starcke, a contemporary American mystic and author of *It's All God*, writes:

> It might shock some to hear it put so bluntly, but Jesus fits the description the dictionary gives for a "mutation." It tells us that a mutation is "a sudden, well-marked transmissible variation in the organism of an animal or plant. A sudden departure from the hereditary background as when an individual differs from its parents." As such, a mutation is not only an extraordinary happening when a new form becomes created but it is also marked by the fact that the new form can be followed by others, that it establishes a whole new being. Jesus not only represented something new for mankind but also he revealed a new dimension that all those who followed him could have.[1]

I want to emphasize that upon the realization of causal consciousness "you" or "I," our human personalities, do not become enlightened. I was asked by a man at a talk I gave if I was enlightened. Although I suspected the man asked this as a sort of trick question meant to throw me off balance, I said yes, meaning that I have realized the Christ Consciousness on a permanent basis. But I suspect that what the man was really asking was if I, Jim Marion the personality, was enlightened (after all, 99.99% of humans think they *are* their space-time personalities and see others in the same light). My answer to that question should have been no.

Saint Paul was trying to get at this when he wrote, "I live, now not I, but Christ lives in me." It is very hard to explain to people who are identified with their egos what life is like when the ego has died. In a sense, *there is no more me* to be enlightened or otherwise. "I" am gone, though, of course, and here is the paradox, I am still here being used as a vessel of the divine. Was Jesus a human personality or incarnate Son of God? The answer is both. He was a human being when seen from a personality perspective and a divine being when seen with the eyes of the Spirit. The same is true of anyone who realizes the Christ Consciousness.

What is true of a person with Christ Consciousness is also true of everybody else—except that everybody else doesn't realize who they are. We think we need to be saved. We don't. We are *already* sons and daughters of God in exactly the same sense that Jesus was—except that he knew who he was and we don't know who we are. When one realizes the Christ Consciousness and "sees" one's union with God, then one sees this truth as clearly as one can hear a ringing bell. It becomes obvious. One sees that one is freed from sin or "saved" (and has always been so). One sees one was never under sin's dominion in the first place. May we all come to that wondrous realization, for that is the truth about which the scripture is speaking in saying that the truth will forever set us free.

The second point I want to emphasize is that the "levels of consciousness" that I have described (from archaic to causal) are levels of *cognitive* development that basically center on one's understanding of self (and later, Self) and our struggle to understand and answer the question "Who am I?" The levels of cognitive development are the ones that are emphasized by almost all mystics and contemplatives and are the ones generally depicted in any description of the spiritual path. There are, however, many other lines of human development such as psychological development, psychosexual development, intellectual development, artistic development, mathematical development, moral development, values development, emotional development, and so forth. There are probably 20 or 30 lines of development in all.

The levels taken from *Spiral Dynamics,* described earlier in this book (beige, purple, red, blue, orange, green, yellow, and turquoise) are levels of *values* development. Lawrence Kohlberg, Carol Gilligan, and others have written of the levels of *moral* development. James Fowler's levels, alluded to earlier, are levels of *faith* development. Though all the various types of levels have similarities (e.g., they evolve in similar fashion from small, narrowly egocentric holons to ever more encompassing holons), they each have their own distinctive learnings and realizations.

So when people ask, "Where am I on the spiritual path?" the question is seldom an easy one to answer. As Wilber says, the self-system is all over the place. One can be at level four in moral development and level two in emotional development and level six in cognitive development. My belief is that the path Jesus taught emphasized both cognitive and emotional development. In other words, Jesus taught that it wasn't enough to be just cognitively enlightened so that one knows one is united with God. Jesus taught that it is also important to be psychologically whole, a human being who has successfully integrated the various parts of self into oneness.

In this I believe Jesus' teachings and example went well beyond those of the Buddha. The Buddha experienced and taught cognitive enlightenment. Jesus, however, taught and expressed not only cognitive enlightenment but also how to love one's neighbor as oneself, an ability that requires psychological wholeness.

I believe that the purpose of the Dark Night of the Soul, which Jesus symbolically demonstrated for us by his Crucifixion and Resurrection, is not only the realization of oneness with God but also the achievement of psychological wholeness. Jesus told many parables that seem to tell us that the goal of the spiritual path is psychological wholeness. For example, in the parable of the weeds and the wheat, Jesus stated that weeds and wheat must be allowed to grow together lest in pulling out weeds, one also pulled out the wheat. He meant that the positive and negative sides of our personalities must be allowed to evolve side by side until, in the Dark Night of the Soul, the negative parts are transmuted into positive.

Jesus also likened the kingdom of heaven to a pearl of great price and to a coin that was lost. Both the pearl and the coin, because of their circular shape, are symbols of wholeness—the circle being the symbol of psychological wholeness in many religions—from the Eucharistic wafer of Christians to the mandalas of Tibetan Buddhists to the medicine wheels of the Native Americans.

In the Gospel of Thomas,[2] Jesus explicitly talks about the necessity of uniting the male and female parts of oneself (as does Saint Paul in saying that in the kingdom of heaven, the Christ Consciousness, there is no male or female). The uniting of our male and female parts results in psychological wholeness.[3] In the Gospel of Thomas, it says:

> Jesus said to them, "When you make the two into one, when you make the inner like the outer and the outer like the inner, and the upper like the lower, when you make male and female into a single one, so that the male will not be male and the female will not be female . . . then you will enter the kingdom."

Though I believe Jesus taught a path that combined cognitive and psychological development, I do not know what that path was in terms of meditation techniques, rituals, or behavioral practices. Jesus' path, which he taught orally and secretly to his disciples, has been lost. It may have survived for a while in the early Church, where a sharp distinction was made between initiates into the Christian mysteries and those who were not yet initiated. Generally, the initiates were sworn to secrecy regarding their practices, which were handed down orally and seldom put in writing.[4]

Jesus' secret teachings may have been of special importance to those early Christians who clearly believed in step-by-step development into a higher consciousness. Those Christians were generally called Gnostics, from the Greek word *gnosis,* meaning "knowledge," especially secret or higher knowledge. But whatever spiritual practices Jesus taught (aside from the external observance of Holy Communion and baptism by water) were apparently lost as Christianity was taken over by people with a decidedly lower level of consciousness (magical and mythic).[5]

The reason I raise these issues here is because I agree with Wilber, who maintains that one can be cognitively enlightened but remain unwhole psychologically. One can complete half of what Jesus preached as enlightenment while missing the other half. Perhaps one can be cognitively enlightened (the goal of Buddhism?) but lack Jesus' ability to love because one is not psychologically whole (having not gone through the Dark Night of the Soul). Like so much else about the higher parts of the spiritual path, there is still much research to be done in answering these questions.

It does seem that some cognitively enlightened gurus apparently think they can do whatever they please and treat their disciples and other people however they please. Some have been authoritarian; some have been sexual abusers; some have used their positions for monetary and social aggrandize-ment. Still others may hold rather ignorant views when it comes to such matters as human sexuality and gender, and still others have been quite neurotic and verbally abusive of others. All of these cognitively enlightened ones are deficient in psychological development, and some of them are deficient in moral and psychosexual development as well.

Of course, some of these so-called enlightened gurus may not be enlightened at all. The late Christian saint, Father Bede Griffiths, O.S.B., who established and led a Christian ashram in India for 40 years, warned mystic Andrew Harvey in late 1992, "Many gurus now are not enlightened beings but black magicians, occult Masters manipulating millions of seekers: what Jesus called 'wolves in sheep's clothing.' All of the serious mystical systems know of the existence of these occult powers, but modern seekers are naïve and uninformed and so vulnerable to them. These 'Masters' are not actually helping the Great Birth but working against it, aborting it."[6]

Harvey writes that he later learned that his own guru, Mother Meera, was such a one, and in recent years extremely serious questions about sexual and other improprieties have been raised concerning Sai Baba, who draws millions to his ashram in India, has the ear of prominent Indian politicians, and supposedly materializes objects out of thin air.

In *Sun at Midnight,* Harvey argues forcefully and convincingly that the contemporary guru scene is deeply corrupted by gurus who are black magicians, that is, unenlightened frauds who use psychic powers to draw and keep disciples and are primarily interested in power, money, sex, and fame. Harvey's account is a terrifying one that shows the lengths some of these black magicians will go to entrap their disciples, enslave them, and threaten them if they try to escape, often using occult powers to send diseases, make death threats, destroy relationships, and all manner of horrors. Along with death threats, Harvey and his partner, Eryk Hanut, had a dead snake delivered to them in the mail and a bomb thrown in their window. Psychic attacks were even made on Hanut's will to live.

Often these gurus teach the common but false doctrine that without a guru there can be no enlightenment. This is both self-serving and untrue. Enlightenment comes from God, not through a guru. Many of them set themselves up to be treated as gods, inaccessible behind a bodyguard of the most loyal and convinced devotees, showered with flowers, sitting on thrones, their every need seen to by slavelike devotees, charging extravagant fees for their workshops and initiations, and so on. Can you imagine Jesus allowing himself to be treated this way?

These gurus have failed the test that Jesus passed in the desert when Jesus refused occult powers. Jesus also refused all earthly power when it was offered to him. Guru-worship may be tradition in the East but it has become a corrupt tradition, open to all manner of abuse, and for Americans and Europeans to submit themselves uncritically to this kind of spiritual enterprise is folly. To go from the sometimes oppressive patriarchy of the Christian Church to slavish devotion to one of these false gurus is to go from the frying pan to the fire.

For my part, I strongly encourage all seekers to forget about gurus, and go directly to God, Jesus, Mary, and the other genuine saints of whatever tradition. Avoid any spiritual movement based upon the glorification of any human, and all spiritual movements with oppressive authority structures. Enlightenment or Christ Consciousness requires that we come into our own divinity, our own power, our own unique human individuation. You cannot become enlightened if you have given away your power by projection onto guru or pope. Spiritual teachers and others can help, but we must do the work ourselves. There is no other way.

I also urge all seekers to work hard on all aspects of their development, particularly on psychological wholeness. I believe that psychological wholeness is every bit as important as cognitive enlightenment and that, to follow the path to the kingdom that Jesus laid out, both types of realization are essential.

Another reason that I think psychological wholeness is so important is because, in my experience, the chief obstacle to higher consciousness for most people is an emotional one. Most of us are weighted down with all kinds of fears, many of which may not even be in our conscious awareness. Fear functions like a dead weight in our psyche, dragging down our level of consciousness and greatly impeding our growth. We want to become psychologically whole so we can *love,* and, as the scriptures say, fear is the chief opponent to love and the biggest obstacle to loving.

Even if one does have both types of realization, cognitive and psychological, that does not mean one is a "perfect" human being (whatever "perfect" may mean). Even enlightened ones have work to do on themselves. Sri Yukteswarji, the teacher of Paramahansa Yogananda, once remarked that "Those who are too good for this world are adorning some other." We are all here to grow as deeply into our divine calling as we can—and space-time is designed to propel us along. The marvelous enlightened mystic Walter Starcke, who has written several wonderful books, writes:

> To be a perfect man, one must have flaws. One must have imperfections to keep one humble, pure and truly man . . . When we realize that imperfections, thorns in the flesh, are part of the perfection of life, we can see that there is no power apart from God. Were there no imperfections, there would be nothing to spur man on to creation. Were there no unfulfilled desire motivating him, man would not move . . . I was given a flaw in my character or life to keep me pushing and creating.[7]

Saint Paul, even though he clearly had the Christ Consciousness, complained of the thorn in his flesh, that is, some fault that he kept repeating. God advised Paul that the fault was necessary to keep him humble and seeking. Many exegetes have wondered if Jesus himself had faults in the human sense of the term. They criticize him for cursing and killing the fig tree, for driving demons into the swine of a farmer so that the swine plunged off a cliff into the sea and were killed, for losing his temper so egregiously with the money lenders in the temple, for his constant annoyance with his apostles because of their denseness, for his extreme attacks on the religious leaders of his religion, and even for being rude to his mother, both at Cana and when she came one day with others to see him. Apparently Jesus, too, as Starcke has noted, may have had his bad days.

In Jesus' case, all of these things, at most, were surface disturbances. Underneath he was perpetually at peace. This is how it usually is at the causal level. Our personalities can still get upset over events, but underneath, at the place where we identify with our divinity, all is well. All any of us can do is to maintain as great a purity of heart and intention as we can and to truly seek to accomplish God's will as best we understand it. In the end, that is enough. The pure of heart will see God. All others will get lost.

Another topic I want to address, in light of the evolutionary theme of this book, is nonduality. The nondual "level" of consciousness, which seems to be generally encountered some years after the realization of the causal level, is not so much a "level" as a direct experience of Spirit as the ground of being, the *suchness,* to use Meister Eckhart's[8] word, of all that is. It is the unification of subject, object, and relationship, for example, Father, Son, and Spirit, knower, known, and knowing. Whereas at the causal level the seeker experiences a "union with" God or Spirit (note the slight duality), in nonduality one experiences *direct identification with* God or Spirit.

155

When Jesus, speaking as the Christ, says, "The Father and I are One," he is expressing his nondual experience. Metaphysically, Jesus' statement is identical to the Buddhist "Nirvana is Samsara" and the Hindu "Brahman is Atman." Jesus is the word of God, the "Word by whom all things were made" (John 1:3), that is, the First Principle of Creation and hence a stand-in for Creation itself. So "The Father and I are One" means that God and Creation are one without a two, made of the same essence and substance. In the Buddhist statement, *nirvana* is said to be the same, that is, made of the same essence as *samsara*—Earth, space-time, creation. In the Hindu statement "Brahman is Atman," Brahman, the Creator, is said to be of the same substance as Atman, the Self, the human soul.

All three metaphysical statements express the nondual realization that God and Creation are of like essence and substance. When a contemplative of any spiritual tradition experiences nonduality, the suchness of what is, he clearly sees that Creation itself is an aspect or manifestation of God. All of Creation is divine. Thus the unfolding of Creation, the evolutionary process, is a divine process. It is God's own unfolding in space-time.

Mythic Christians believe that, though Jesus was divine, the rest of humanity is not (and, by extension, creation itself certainly is not). As the Catholic woman reader who wrote to me said, a divine being, the Christ, had to be sent down from the sky to restore us to grace because "there is nothing man can do to get it [grace], or to get it back." Only a divine being could appease God and restore us to grace after the "fall" of Adam and Eve. This, however, is almost tantamount to saying that Jesus was not a human being but a god, someone radically and essentially different from the rest of us, and that his birth constituted a radical "supernatural intervention" on God's part into the evolutionary process.[9] In my judgment, this view almost completely denigrates Jesus' humanity.

At the other extreme are certain modern attempts to start from the bottom up by accepting the fact that Jesus was a human and to try to explain his divinity as symbolic. One such attempt was recently made by the American Jesuit, green, postmodern theologian Roger Haight in his book *Jesus, Symbol of God.* Father Haight argues that, in Jesus, God broke through to us in a special way, showed His nature in a special way, manifested Himself in a special way. All that is true enough, but Father Haight seems to have trouble accepting the traditional Christian Creed that Jesus was made of the same essence and substance as God. In other words, Father Haight seems to have gone to the other extreme, underemphasizing Jesus' divinity.

In my judgment both views are incomplete. When Jesus, speaking as the Christ, the Word from which all else of Creation was made (John 1:3), says, "The Father and I are One," the Gospel means that all of us and all creation are one with God, divine in precisely the same sense that Jesus was. All of Creation, including ourselves, is made of the substance and essence of God. We are all birthed of God; we are all begotten, not made; we are all light of light; and we are all of one being with the Father. He who sees us sees God, just as Jesus said. This is not only the primary realization of the nondual level, but it is also the essential "Good News" of the Gospel itself.

Christianity spread like wildfire in the early centuries because it told even slaves that they were not mere humans but sons and daughters of God Himself and joint heirs with Jesus to the kingdom. Unfortunately, only those humans who, like Jesus, have evolved into the Christ Consciousness and nondual levels can "see" this clearly for themselves. Only they can see the reality of our divinity with their everyday consciousness. Only they, like the late great Mother Teresa of Calcutta, can truly see everyone as the divine Christ they actually are.

The Death of the Mythic God

Neither mythic Christians at the blue level nor postmodern theologians at the green have gone deep enough within themselves to find out who they are. But whether we can see it or not, the reality of our divinity is the Christian belief and, sadly, one that is not understood by both mythic believers and most postmodern thinkers.

There are exceptions. Postmodern American theologian Matthew Fox, the founder of the University of Creation Spirituality in Oakland, California, has been preaching about the sacredness of humanity and of the Earth and all Creation for the last 20 years. In book after book, such as *The Coming of the Cosmic Christ, Original Blessing: A Primer in Creation Spirituality*, and *Creativity: Where the Divine and Human Meet*, Fox has been setting forth his vision of the divinity of humans and Creation. He has been a magnificent and prophetic voice, and he has made no secret of the fact that his great mentor is the great nondual mystic Meister Eckhart.

Where does the realization of our divinity lead us? It leads me, at least, to affirm the words of President John F. Kennedy when he said, "Here on Earth God's work must truly be our own." God is never going to intervene supernaturally on this Earth no matter how many times we beg God to do so. If miracles happen, they will happen because of our own faith, not because of God's intervention. So we have to be God's eyes, ears, arms, legs, and brains on this planet. If the kingdom of heaven is to be realized on Earth, it is up to us, each and every one of us, to make it happen. It is not going to happen by itself.

I agree entirely with Ken Wilber, Walter Starcke, and Andrew Cohen (see his books *Embracing Heaven and Earth* and *Living Enlightenment*) that the old spiritual emphasis on fleeing this world has had its day in both the West and the East. It no longer serves us. We should not see the Earth, nor our bodies, nor our sexuality, nor our everyday occupations as "second-best." We do not need to flee this world. We are called to manifest the kingdom of heaven right here, right now. We are called to divinize everything about our humanity and our role in the evolutionary process. We are called to be gods upon the Earth, just as Jesus prophesied. I hope we will all answer our calling.

Conclusion

In this book I have tried to show that Christianity is today in a period of profound spiritual crisis. It is a crisis that is far more serious than the one that gave rise to the Protestant Reformation five hundred years ago or the splitting of the Eastern and Western branches of the Church a thousand years ago. Moreover, since Christianity has been the principal spiritual expression of the West for almost two thousand years, the crisis in Christianity is having a profound effect on Western culture in general.

I have argued that at the root of this crisis is the core question: Does God exist? For at least 125 years now, the West has been debating the death of God. God's death was first proclaimed by the philosopher Nietzsche and other members of the intelligentsia, particularly by scientists. Now millions in the West have become atheist or agnostic or have been practicing

Christianity largely for reasons of social respectability. Now even the latter reason for attending church or believing in God is largely losing its effectiveness. As a result, all the mainstream churches are in a period of accelerated decline.

What I have tried to demonstrate is that it is not God who has died but a particular conception of God, a mythic conception of God. Until the Age of Reason and the rise of modern science, beginning with Copernicus and Galileo, the consciousness of most Christians was at what many contemporary scholars call the mythic level of consciousness. Christians at the mythic level of consciousness believed in a mythic God. The mythic God lived in the heavens above the vault (ceiling) of the stars. He was a being separate and apart from humans, who created the physical universe and who would intervene in this world whenever summoned to do so by prayer. His biggest intervention was to send his divine son down from heaven to sacrifice himself for the sins of humans.

The mythic God has been dying in the West for five hundred years due to the advances in one science after another. Astronomy has destroyed the beliefs in heaven as a place and in the Earth as special in the eyes of God. Psychology has shown that the demons of earlier ages can better be understood as mental illnesses. Biblical criticism has restored the humanness of Jesus and has shown that the Bible could not possibly be historically true in hundreds of instances. Biology, geology, and archeology have discovered the great truth of evolution. Humans were not created by God in Eden but evolved from lesser animals over eons.

These are just a few of the ways that science has undermined belief in a mythic God. The Church, for its part, has made matters worse by opposing one scientific advance after another and by colossal failures of moral leadership. It has made matters worse by its oppression of women, homosexuals, and, in the past, people of African and aboriginal descent. It has made matters worse by continuing to preach belief in a mythic God, one who was deaf to Auschwitz and all the other great horrors of the last century. Finally, the Church has made matters worse by neglecting almost entirely the preaching of the kingdom of heaven within ourselves that Jesus gave his life trying to show us.

Now that the mythic God has largely died in the West, I have suggested that the mythic God be replaced by the God that can only be found by going within the self. I have tried to show that this was indeed the "Father" that Jesus preached and that Jesus himself did not believe in a God who was external to humankind. I have tried to urge us all to undertake the difficult work of inner growth in consciousness, the same task that Jesus demanded of us.

What might we discover if we enter this inner world? The second half of the book explored the levels of consciousness above the mythic level. It explored the pluses and minuses of each level. It also set out some of the spiritual powers and realizations a person is likely to encounter along the way of inner growth. Finally, I set forth the goal of inner growth: the realization of causal or Christ Consciousness. At that level any idea of a God separate from humans disappears entirely. We finally see that we are divine beings, not mere human beings. We can say with Jesus, "He who sees me sees the Father."

Once we realize our divinity we also realize that no outside God is ever going to intervene to solve the problems of this planet. Relying on our inner guidance from the God within, we must solve these problems ourselves. The more people realize this—and the sooner—the quicker we can all get on with the huge tasks before us. I wish each person well in taking on the colossal spiritual challenge that faces us all.

Afterword
What Should I Do?

Many people have written to me after reading *Putting on the Mind of Christ,* and one of the most common questions is "What should I do to progress along the spiritual path to higher consciousness?" Many people have asked me to recommend various meditation techniques or other spiritual practices. So I thought I would conclude this book by writing a few things about spiritual practice.

If I were the contemporary Indian teacher Sri Sri Ravi Shankar, I would recommend the yoga technique he teaches, *sudarshan kriya.* If I were a member of Yogananda's Self-Realization organization, I would recommend the *kriya* he taught. If I were a parish priest, I would recommend, first and foremost, daily Mass and Communion. There are hundreds of different spiritual practices I could recommend. I could tell you about my own favorite practices and techniques, practices that have varied considerably over the years. But I do not know what would be best for you. Remember, one of the things you are doing at the higher levels of the spiritual life is becoming an individuated human, a unique flower in God's beautiful garden. No one is alike, especially at the higher levels of consciousness. So to a large extent each of us has to follow our own path.

However, I would definitely recommend meditation, for, as Wilber notes, meditation is the only technique that has been scientifically proven to raise the consciousness levels of adults. All of the major spiritual traditions, East and West, are highly reliant upon meditation. So I would say meditation is an absolute must if one expects to realize higher consciousness. Even Jesus often went off alone to meditate away from the crowds and even the demands of the disciples.

But I believe that more important than anything else in realizing higher consciousness is not one's practices but one's *intent*. Jesus promised that those who truly ask will surely find—provided we want God, as Jesus said, with all our heart and soul and mind and strength. One of my favorite stories is about the spiritual master who waded with his disciple into a lake. The master then had his disciple take a deep breath and put his head under water. Then the master held the disciple's head under the water. Eventually, the disciple, who felt he couldn't hold his breath any longer, began to squirm. The master still held his head under the water. Finally, the disciple began thrashing about wildly and broke free, grasping for air. The master said, "When you want God as much as you just wanted air, then you will have a chance at enlightenment."

Our intent is the most important thing, and it needs to be a ferocious intent. Jesus emphasized this often. He said that if one's eye gets in your way, then pluck it out. If one's hand gets in the way, then cut it off. He told the young man to get rid of all his wealth and other attachments. He told another man not to bother burying his father but to let the dead bury the dead. He refused to let family or other relationship ties get in the way. Over and over again, Jesus emphasized that, if you want God, all else must be secondary—family, property, worldly obligations, everything. God must know that you are serious, and, if you are serious, the way will open for you.

If you ask for help and guidance toward liberation, then that help and guidance will come into your life, often from unexpected sources and directions. You will find the practice that suits you best at this particular time. You will encounter the people who will help you most. You will find the books and healing you need. If you are serious. And if you put God first in your life and subordinate all else to your search for God.

So that is my advice. Put God first. Be willing to sacrifice everything else to realize your divinity—everything else. Do this with a ferocious intent. Think about it and act upon it every day from the first thing upon waking to the last thing before going to bed. Seek God, God, God. If you do, you will succeed— and all else will be added. May the peace that surpasses all understanding be with you all.

Endnotes

Introduction to Part I

1. I am not suggesting that an infant is selfish in a moral sense. I am not making moral judgments, just describing "what is."

2. Even, some would say unfortunately, some native psychic (or ESP) abilities.

3. Moses' Ten Commandments had been preceded by the code of laws issued by the Babylonian king Hammurabi (about 1750 B.C.E.) and were followed by that of Solon in Greece (about 600 B.C.E.). Thus the rise of mythic consciousness was not unique to the Hebrews.

4. Water is H_2O in India and America. It flows downhill, per gravity, everywhere. It freezes at 32 degrees Fahrenheit everywhere. These examples show how crucial the development of science and the discovery of science's universal laws were to the development in the West of a rational, universal consciousness and worldview.

5. Ironically, as we have just seen, the fundamentalists, whom I so strongly criticize in this book, were at the cutting edge of human consciousness when the last great leap was made. Again

ironically, yesteryear's cutting edge can become today's force of darkness.

6. *Washington Times*, October 17, 2003, p. A6.

7. *Washington Post*, Nov. 22, 2003, p. A6. Bush was actually theologically correct, for the Koran explicitly states that Muslims worship the God of Noah, Abraham, and Jesus.

Chapter 1

1. Friedrich Nietzsche, *The Gay Science*, Section 126, 1882.

2. Friedrich Nietzsche, *The Gay Science*, 2d edition, Section 243, 1887.

3. The science of the time held that only the male seed was necessary for human conception, nothing being contributed by the woman. The woman was seen as merely the receptacle of the male seed and the incubator of the fetus.

4. Cited in Peter Russell, *From Science to God*, Las Vegas, Nev., Elf Rock, 2002, p. 24.

5. Cited in Richard Tarnas, *The Passion of the Western Mind*, New York, Harmony Books, 1991, pp. 252-3.

6. James Usher (1580-1656), the Church of England's archbishop of Armagh in Ireland, used the genealogies in the Bible to calculate the age of the Earth and of humankind. He figured these to be exactly 4,004 years. Even today some fundamentalist Christians adhere to Usher's chronology.

7. In 1996, after the evolutionary hypothesis had been corroborated by dozens of sciences (such as geology, paleontology, biology, astronomy, genetics, archeology, and so on), Pope John Paul II finally acknowledged that the theory of evolution was "more than just an hypothesis."

8. Northern and southern branches of Presbyterianism reunited in 1983.

9. William Lee Miller, *Arguing about Slavery: The Great Battle in the United States Congress*, New York, Knopf, 1996, p.139.

10. Dunbar Rowland, *Jefferson Davis*, volume 1, New York, AMS Press, 1973, p. 286.

11. Pius IX, Instruction of June 20, 1866, cited in J. F. Maxwell, "The Development of Catholic Doctrine Concerning Slavery," *World Jurist* 11 (1969-70), pp. 306-307.

12. Pius, though he may have thought he was doing so, was not defending the core doctrines of Christianity. Instead, he was defending a particular historical, intellectual, and cultural worldview in which those doctrines had become enmeshed, a worldview that was under siege from every direction.

Most of the sentiments, assumptions, and judgments of the *Syllabus* were repudiated by the Second Vatican Council (1962–1965).

13. Pius had some reason to be angry. He began his pontificate as a reformer and appointed a lay prime minister to carry them out. But in 1848, his prime minister was assassinated by revolutionaries, and he, traumatized, had to flee Rome.

14. In a notorious 1858 incident, Pius had his papal troops kidnap from his parents six-year-old Edgardo Mortara, a Jewish boy whom Pius had heard someone had secretly baptized. He had the boy raised Catholic. When Protestant heads of state objected, Pius, citing a "Protestant conspiracy," slapped draconian restrictions on the Jews of Rome.

15. Pope John Paul II beatified Pius IX in September 2000, the last step before canonization as a saint, which Pius certainly was not.

16. Infallibility, as defined by the Council, has been exercised only once since 1869: by the promulgation of the doctrine of the Assumption of Mary into heaven by Pius XII in 1950.

17. The closest to what historically happened is probably the very first scriptural account, that of Paul. Paul, like the Creed, simply says Jesus was buried. No Joseph of Arimathea getting a special tomb. No rolled-back stone. No angels. No missing body. But after Jesus' death and burial, he appeared in visions of some sort to many, including Paul himself. (I discuss these visions at length in *Putting on the Mind of Christ.*)

18. Pius X, Motu Proprio *Sacrorum Antistitum,* September 1, 1910. (Pius XII finally approved biblical criticism in 1943 in the encyclical *Divino Afflante Spiritu,* and the oath was dropped in 1967.)

19. Catholics also believed in purgatory, a "place" where one stayed after death for a *certain duration of time* to be purified before entering heaven.

Chapter 2

1. The American Jesuit theologian Gustave Weigel quipped that Vatican II brought the Church forward by centuries—to the eighteenth (cited in Robert Blair Kaiser, *Clerical Error,* New York, Continuum, 2002, p. 159).

2. Nietzsche, *The Gay Science,* section 125, 1882.

3. Nietzsche, *The Gay Science,* section 343, 2d edition, 1887.

4. Pentecostal churches, though mainly fundamentalist, preach a direct experiential relationship with God, a feature they have in common with the New Age movement, which is also growing.

5. "Religious Congregations and Membership: 2000," *Washington Post,* Sept. 17, 2002.

6. Thomas C. Reeves, *The Empty Church: Does Organized Religion Really Matter Anymore?* New York, Simon & Schuster, 1998; cited online at www.religioustolerance.org.

7. Laurie Goodstein, "As Attacks' Impact Recedes, a Return to Religion as Usual," *New York Times,* Nov. 26, 2001.

8. I am not in favor of abortion. To abort the life plans of another soul is to incur serious negative karma. But neither, as a matter of public policy, do I want women and doctors made into criminals for doing what the Church judges wrong. Let the Church issue moral guidance, but let women make their own choices, and let the state and its criminal law stay out of people's intimate moral choices.

9. Alan Cooperman, "Rift in Lutheran Denomination Deepens," *Washington Post,* July 20, 2002.

10. Rev. Benke's suspension was later overturned by a three-person appeals panel.

11. PBS has reported that scientists think they may have discovered the ruins of Sodom, burnt bricks and all. The geologic and archeological evidence suggests an earthquake that released and ignited gases trapped in the Earth. This fireball, in turn, ignited the small sulfur balls which are ubiquitous in the region, thus causing a "hail" of fire. "The Dead Sea," aired on WETA, Washington, D.C., Sept. 15, 2002.

12. Nietzsche, *The Gay Science,* section 125, 1882.

Chapter 3

1. John Shelby Spong, *A New Christianity for a New World,* HarperSanFrancisco, 2001, pp. 21–22.

2. Some late medieval popes went even further, asserting jurisdiction even over the world of the dead. In order to raise revenues to build palaces and churches in Rome, they began granting indulgences of days and months off from one's temporal sentence to purgatory in exchange for money, a scandalous practice that eventually helped precipitate the Protestant revolt.

3. Jesus, of course, is speaking of a spiritual sword (i.e., troubles). In Luke 22:36, and in Matthew 26:52 after Peter had cut off the ear of the High Priest's slave, Jesus tells Peter to put back his sword and that those who take up the sword are destroyed by it. Boniface was eager to use what Jesus had forbidden to be used.

4. The Orthodox church, of course, is equally patriarchal though with less grand "supernatural" pretensions.

5. Beatrice Bruteau, *God's Ecstasy: The Creation of a Self-Creating World,* New York, Crossroad, 1997, pp. 55–56.

6. Samaritans were Jews but were considered heretics by the Pharisees and Sadducees.

Chapter 4

1. Gilles Farcet, editor, *Radical Awakening: Cutting through the Conditioned Mind: Dialogues with Stephen Jourdain,* Carlsbad, Calif., Inner Directions, 2001, p. 135.

2. "Man in 'The Image of the Heavenly'" from *Treasures from the Writings of Jacob Boehme,* online at www.passtheword.org/Jacob-Boehme.

3. The Hindu "Brahman is Atman" (roughly, "God is the True Self") and the Buddhist "Nirvana is Samsara" (roughly, "heaven is Earth") have the same meaning as Jesus' "The Father and I are one." They all express the relationship of Creator to Creation *and* the oneness of Creator and Creation.

4. Bruteau, *God's Ecstasy,* p. 9.

Introduction to Part II

1. This applies to other traditions as well but is especially evident in Christianity.

Chapter 5

1. According to Plato, almost everything in space-time was seen as a reflection of an "ideal form" at the causal level. This was a static nonevolutionary idea. What exists at the causal level might be better understood as the "pool of all potentialities" (together with certain principles such as those of mathematics), not the elaborated forms that are produced, and are being produced, by the evolutionary process itself.

2. "Spin" is a fundamental property of nature like mass or electrical charge. Protons, neutrons, and electrons have spin.

3. David Bohm, *Wholeness and the Implicate Order,* London and New York, Routledge, 1980, pp. 71–72.

4. One example might be the soul, which exists at the causal level, and its many incarnations, which exist primarily at the physical and astral/subtle levels. This insight also has implications for what we call "evolution."

Chapter 6

1. Bruteau, *God's Ecstasy,* p. 12.

2. Here I am writing of God as Source (the Father in Christian mythology) and God as Creation (the Son in Christian mythology) as two. Earlier I quoted Jesus' saying the "the Father and I are one" (nirvana is samsara, Brahman is Atman). Both statements are true. Creation and Source are ontologically the same yet different. To our rational minds these truths constitute a paradox that cannot be adequately explained in words. At the causal level of consciousness, however, one can clearly see the truth of both statements and that they do not contradict each other. One sees this, of course, with one's inner vision, the eye of contemplation, as I earlier called that vision.

3. Bruteau, *God's Ecstasy,* p. 44.

4. Rupert Sheldrake, *A New Science of Life: The Hypothesis of Morphic Resonance,* Rochester, Vt., Park Street Press, 1995.

5. Sheldrake insists that the morphic fields are not "metaphysical," that is, "above or outside of the physical world." Yet, clearly, they are above and/or outside what we normally define as space-time. They are, in effect, subtle energy fields that are physical in such a highly refined sense that we could just as accurately label them as

spiritual. See Wilber on the shambhala.com website for a further elaboration of such subtle physical energies.

Chapter 7

1. In Fowler, the archaic level is called that of "undifferentiated faith." The magical level is called that of "intuitive/projective faith," and the mythic level "mythic/literal faith." Evolution in consciousness, of course, affects a person's entire worldview, but Fowler is especially concerned with religious attitudes and religious worldview.

2. *Washington Post,* October 22, 2003, p. A12.

3. Eckhart Tolle, *The Power of Now: A Guide to Spiritual Enlightenment,* Novato, Calif., New World Library, 1999, p. 67.

4. Ibid., p. 13.

Chapter 8

1. Mythic consciousness and rational consciousness are also mental levels of awareness.

2. Earlier levels are called by other colors; for example, the rational level is orange, the mythic blue, and the magical purple.

3. Ken Wilber, *Boomeritis: A Novel That Will Set You Free,* Boston, Shambhala, 2002, p. 27.

4. The green *Washington Post* ran story after story on the pedophilia scandal—in lurid pornographic detail.

5. American elections cost millions of dollars because of the expense of TV advertisements. Congress could remedy the need for these monies by requiring the TV stations that hold licenses to the public airways to broadcast such ads free of charge as a public service. But then, under the Constitution, third parties would also have to be afforded free advertising, and neither the Republicans nor Democrats want to allow that. So the influence of big money continues.

Chapter 10

1. The Jew will not utter God's name. The Muslim allows no image of God. The Buddhist will not even speak of God. For good reason: None want to repeat the Christian experience in which none of these strictures are followed and people talk endlessly about "god" and what God is like or not like, what God approves or doesn't approve,

and so forth, with the result that most Christians end up worshiping not the real God about whom little can be said, but a product of their own imagination and projection, that is, an idol or false god.

2. I reserve the word "saint" for those who are enlightened, those at the Christ Consciousness or causal level, a level Wilber calls the level of sages.

3. Einstein was a citizen of both Switzerland and the United States.

4. Biographies are available on the Internet.

5. By "revealed scripture," I mean a text written by a person with causal (Christ) consciousness or at least "channeled" or "inspired" from that level of awareness.

6. In his autobiography, Paramahansa Yogananda tells of the Indian saint Trailanga, whom a skeptic offered a bowl of calcium-lime instead of clabbered milk. Trailanga suffered no ill effect after ingesting it, but the skeptic fell to the ground in agony. Trailanga said, "You did not realize when you offered me poison that my life is one with your own. Except for my knowledge that God is present in my stomach as in every atom of creation, the lime would have killed me." *Autobiography of a Yogi,* Los Angeles, Self-Realization Fellowship, 1990, p. 331. Cf. also the story of Elijah and the she-bear.

Chapter 11

1. Gregg Braden, *The Isaiah Effect,* New York, Harmony Books, 2000, p. 163.

2. Ibid., p.164.

3. Ibid., p. 167.

4. David Spangler, *The Laws of Manifestation,* Scotland, Findhorn, 1983, pp. 4–5.

5. Ibid., pp. 5–6.

6. Ibid., p. 15.

Chapter 12

1. God, of course, cannot be offended. Only the false, anthropomorphic, projected "God" of the mythic level can be offended, angry, pleased, appeased, or subject to other human emotions and motivations.

2. Karma may be simple, but how it interacts with God's mercy is another matter. God no doubt settles for a lot less than "an eye for an eye and a tooth for a tooth," especially when there has been a real conversion and growth in awareness.

3. Daniel Curzon, "Why I Am An Ex-Catholic," in *ReCreations: Religion and Spirituality in the Lives of Queer People,* edited by Catherine Lake, Toronto, Queer Press, 1999, p. 104.

4. I have heard that Pope John Paul II is bitterly disappointed that Poland has not led a general Catholic revival in Eastern Europe, one resulting in a new flowering of (mythic) Christianity, which the Pope apparently fully expected. Instead, church attendance is falling, seminaries are emptying, and the pedophilia scandal has already caused the resignation of one archbishop. Poland is quickly following the rest of Europe into the postmodern rational era.

5. Babies (or adults) are not relieved of original sin by being sprinkled, doused, or immersed in water. Baptism by water is symbolic, not magical. Only Baptism by Spirit in the Dark Night of the Soul (see *Putting on the Mind of Christ*) can relieve us once and for all of our negative karmic inheritance. It is not Jesus of Nazareth's historical death on the cross, but only baptism into Jesus' death (death to the ego) and rebirth into Christ Consciousness that frees us, once and for all, from negative karma (or "sin").

6. Neither can adults who have not realized Christ Consciousness as Jesus explicitly taught, cf. John 3:3.

7. *Sub specie aeternitatis,* that is, from the viewpoint of eternity (and God) there are no accidents and nothing happens by chance. But in space-time, chance and randomness are necessary for evolution to unfold.

8. Despite my attempt to describe clearly the Dark Night of the Soul in *Putting on the Mind of Christ*, many readers have continued to apply the term to any prolonged period of spiritual suffering. I will grant that such a period of prolonged suffering may be described as *a* Dark Night of the Soul but is not necessarily *the* Dark Night of the Soul as described by John of the Cross or me. If the ego has not died and the person has not been resurrected into causal consciousness, then it was not *the* Dark Night of the Soul.

Chapter 13

1. Walter Starcke, *The Double Thread*, Boerne, Tex., Guadalupe Press, 1967, pp. 11–12.

2. The Gospel of Thomas was often mentioned in early Christian writings but no copy was found until 1945. Most biblical scholars seem to agree that it is an authentic gospel, not a later fanciful fabrication.

3. The principal spiritual purpose of sexuality, particularly within a committed, long-term spiritual partnership, is to foster and accelerate the realization of such wholeness.

4. In 1958, a letter from Clement of Alexandria (second century) was found that contained a few passages from a "secret" Gospel of Mark that was available only to initiates. The passages refer to some kind of "baptismal" ritual supposedly used by Jesus to initiate disciples. There is debate about whether the ritual may have involved sexual practices similar to those of other mystery religions of the era. We do not know.

5. These exoteric Christians (people who emphasized externals over internals) actually persecuted, vilified, and condemned their Gnostic brethren and burned their books. Typical mythic-level behavior.

6. Andrew Harvey, *Sun at Midnight: A Memoir of the Dark Night*, New York, Jeremy P. Tarcher/Putnam, 2002, p. 34.

7. Starcke, *The Double Thread*, p. 91.

8. Meister Eckhart (1260–1328), a medieval priest and philosopher, is perhaps the most brilliant Christian mystic who has ever lived.

9. As I explained earlier, God has never supernaturally intervened in the evolutionary process and never will. The process itself springs forth from God and evolves per the Spirit's own unfolding. It needs no outside intervention.

Bibliography

Armstong, Karen. 1993. *A History of God: The 4,000-Year Quest of Judaism, Christianity, and Islam*. New York: Knopf.

Beck, Don Edward, and Christopher C. Cowan. 1996. *Spiral Dynamics: Mastering Values, Leadership, and Change*. Cambridge, Mass.: Blackwell Business.

Bohm, David. 1980, 2002. *Wholeness and the Implicate Order*. New York: Routledge.

Braden, Gregg. 2000. *The Isaiah Effect: Decoding the Lost Science of Prayer and Prophecy*. New York: Harmony Books.

Bruteau, Beatrice. 1971. *Worthy Is the World: The Hindu Philosophy of Sri Aurobindo*. Rutherford, N.J.: Fairleigh Dickinson University Press.

————. 1974. *Evolution toward Divinity: Teilhard de Chardin and the Hindu Traditions.* Wheaton, Ill.: Theosophical Publishing House.

————. 1997. *God's Ecstasy: The Creation of a Self-Creating World.* New York: Crossroad.

————. 2001. *The Grand Option: Personal Transformation and a New Creation.* Notre Dame, Ind.: University of Notre Dame Press.

Cather, Willa, and Georgine Milmine. 1993 [1909]. *The Life of Mary Baker G. Eddy and the History of Christian Science.* Lincoln, Nebr.: University of Nebraska Press.

Cohen, Andrew. 2000. *Embracing Heaven and Earth: The Liberation Teachings of Andrew Cohen.* Lenox, Mass.: Moksha.

————. 2002. *Living Enlightenment: A Call for Evolution beyond Ego.* Lenox, Mass.: Moksha.

Eddy, Mary Baker. 2000 [1875]. *Science and Health: With Key to the Scriptures,* authorized edition. Boston: Writings of Mary Baker Eddy.

Farcet, Gilles (ed.). 2001. *Radical Awakening: Cutting through the Conditioned Mind, Dialogues with Stephen Jourdain.* Carlsbad, Calif.: Inner Directions.

Fillmore, Charles. 1986. *Christian Healing.* Unity Village, Mo.: Unity.

————. 1996. *Jesus Christ Heals.* Unity Village, Mo.: Unity.

————. 1997. *Teach Us to Pray.* Unity Village, Mo.: Unity.

———. 1998. *Prosperity.* Unity Village, Mo.: Unity.

Fowler, James A. 1995. *Stages of Faith: The Psychology of Human Development and the Quest for Meaning.* San Francisco: HarperSanFrancisco.

———. 2000. *Becoming Adult, Becoming Christian: Adult Development and Christian Faith.* San Francisco: Jossey-Bass.

Fox, Matthew. 1980. *Breakthrough: Meister Eckhart's Creation Spirituality, in New Translation.* Garden City, N.Y.: Doubleday.

———. 1983. *Original Blessing: A Primer in Creation Spirituality.* Santa Fe, N.M.: Bear & Co.

———. 1988. *The Coming of the Cosmic Christ: The Healing of Mother Earth and the Birth of a Global Renaissance.* San Francisco: Harper & Row.

———. 1991. *Creation Spirituality: Liberating Gifts for the Peoples of the Earth.* San Francisco: HarperSanFrancisco.

———. 1996. *Confessions: The Making of a Postdenominational Priest.* San Francisco: HarperSanFrancisco.

Gebser, Jean. 1985. *The Ever-Present Origin.* Translated by Noel Barstad. Athens, Ohio: Ohio University Press.

Ghose, Aurobindo. 1982. *The Future Evolution of Man.* Pondicherry, India: Sri Aurobindo Association.

———. 1984. *The Synthesis of Yoga.* Pondicherry, India, Sri Aurobindo Association.

Gilligan, Carol. 1993. *In a Different Voice: Psychological Theory and Women's Development.* Cambridge, Mass.: Harvard University Press.

Goswami, Amit. 1993. *The Self-Aware Universe.* New York: G.P. Putnam's Sons.

Haight, Roger, 1999. *Jesus: Symbol of God.* Maryknoll, N.Y.: Orbis Books.

Harvey, Andrew (ed.). 1997. *The Essential Gay Mystics.* San Francisco: HarperSanFrancisco.

Harvey, Andrew. 1998. *Son of Man: The Mystical Path to Christ.* New York: Jeremy P. Tarcher/Putnam.

———. 2000. *The Direct Path: Creating a Journey to the Divine through the World's Mystical Traditions.* New York: Broadway Books.

———. 2000. *The Return of the Mother.* New York: Jeremy P. Tarcher/Putnam.

———. 2002. *Sun at Midnight: A Memoir of the Dark Night.* New York: Jeremy P. Tarcher/Putnam.

Holmes, Ernest. 1997. *The Science of Mind.* New York: G.P. Putnam's Sons.

Hopkins, Emma Curtis. 1974. *Scientific Christian Mental Practice.* Marina del Rey, Calif.: DeVorss.

Huxley, Aldous. 1945. *The Perennial Philosophy.* New York: Harper.

John of the Cross. 1991. *The Dark Night, The Ascent of Mount Carmel, The Spiritual Canticle, The Living Flame of Love in the Collected Works of Saint John of the Cross.* Translated by Kieran Kavanaugh, OCD, and Otilio Rodriguez, OCD. Washington, D.C.: ICS Publications, Institute of Carmelite Studies.

Keating, Thomas, OCSO. 1992. *Invitation to Love: The Way of Christian Contemplation.* Rockport, Mass.: Element.

———. 1994. *Intimacy with God.* New York: Crossroad.

Keyes, Ken, Jr. 1989. *Handbook to Higher Consciousness.* Coos Bay, Ore.: Love Line Books.

Kohlberg, Lawrence. 1981. *Essays on Moral Development.* San Francisco: Harper.

———. 1981. *The Meaning and Measurement of Moral Development.* Worcester, Mass.: Clark University Heinz Werner Institute.

Kramer, Linda. 2000. *The Religion That Kills: Christian Science: Abuse, Neglect, and Mind Control.* Lafayette, La.: Huntington House.

Laszlo, Ervin. 1987. *Evolution: The Grand Synthesis.* Boston: New Science Library.

Loevinger, Jane. 1976. *Ego Development.* San Francisco: Jossey-Bass.

Morwood, Michael. 1997. *Tomorrow's Catholic: Understanding God and Jesus in a New Millennium.* Mystic, Conn.: Twenty-Third Publications.

———. 2001. *Is Jesus God? Finding Our Faith.* New York: Crossroad.

Murphy, Michael. 1992. *The Future of the Body: Explorations into the Future Evolution of Human Nature.* Los Angeles: Jeremy P. Tarcher.

Nenneman, Richard A. 1997. *Persistent Pilgrim: The Life of Mary Baker Eddy.* Etna, N.H.: Nebbadoon.

Neumann, Erich. 1993. *The Origins and History of Consciousness.* Princeton, N.J.: Princeton University Press.

Peale, Norman Vincent. 1996. *The Power of Positive Thinking.* New York: Ballantine.

Peel, Robert. 1966. *Mary Baker Eddy: The Years of Discovery.* New York: Holt, Rinehart & Winston.

———. 1971. *Mary Baker Eddy: The Years of Trial.* New York: Holt, Rinehart & Winston.

———. 1977. *Mary Baker Eddy: The Years of Authority.* Boston: Christian Science Publishing Society.

Pennington, M. Basil, OCSO. 1982. *Centering Prayer: Renewing an Ancient Christian Prayer Form.* Garden City, N.Y.: Image.

———. 1995. *Call to the Center: The Gospel's Invitation to Deeper Prayer.* Hyde Park, N.Y.: New City Press.

Piaget, Jean. 1997. *The Child's Conception of the World.* Translated by Joan and Andrew Tomlinson. New York: Routledge.

———. 1997. *The Moral Judgment of the Child.* Translated by Marjorie Gabain and William Damon. Glencoe, Ill.: Free Press.

Piaget, Jean, and Barbel Inhelder. 1969. *The Psychology of the Child.* Translated by Helen Weaver. New York: Basic Books.

Quinn, John R. 1999. *The Reform of the Papacy: The Costly Call to Christian Unity.* New York: Crossroad.

Ruether, Rosemary Radford. 2000. *Christianity and the Making of the Modern Family.* Boston: Beacon.

Russell, Peter. 2002. *From Science to God: The Mystery of Consciousness and the Meaning of Light.* Las Vegas, Nev.: Elf Rock.

Sanford, John A. 1978. *Dreams and Healing.* New York: Paulist Press.

———. 1980. *Invisible Partners: How the Male and Female in Each of Us Affects Our Relationships.* New York: Paulist Press.

———. 1981. *Evil: The Shadow Side of Reality.* New York: Crossroad.

———. 1987. *The Kingdom Within: The Inner Meaning of Jesus' Sayings.* San Francisco: Harper & Row.

———. 1989. *Dreams: God's Forgotten Language.* San Francisco: Harper & Row.

Segal, Suzanne. 1998. *Collision with the Infinite: A Life beyond the Personal Self.* San Diego, Calif.: Blue Dove Press.

Sheldrake, Rupert. 1989. *The Presence of the Past: Morphic Resonance and the Habits of Nature.* New York: Vintage Books.

———. 1995. *A New Science of Life: The Hypothesis of Morphic Resonance.* Rochester, Vt.: Park Street Press.

Spangler, David. 1975. *The Laws of Manifestation.* Scotland: Findhorn.

———. 1996. *Everyday Miracles: The Inner Art of Manifestation.* New York: Bantam.

Spong, John Shelby. 1998. *Why Christianity Must Change or Die: A Bishop Speaks to Believers in Exile.* San Francisco: HarperSanFrancisco.

———. 2001. *A New Christianity for a New World: Why Traditional Faith Is Dying and How a New Faith Is Being Born.* San Francisco: HarperSanFrancisco.

Starcke, Walter. 1967. *The Double Thread.* Boerne, Tex.: Guadalupe Press.

———. 1988. *Homesick for Heaven: You Don't Have to Wait.* Boerne, Tex.: Guadalupe Press.

———. 1989. *The Gospel of Relativity.* Boerne, Tex.: Guadalupe Press.

———. 1989. *The Ultimate Revolution: A Spiritual Awakening.* Boerne, Tex.: Guadalupe Press.

———. 1998. *It's All God.* Boerne, Tex.: Guadalupe Press.

Tarnas, Richard. 1991. *The Passion of the Western Mind*. New York: Harmony Books.

Teilhard de Chardin, Pierre. 1959. *The Phenomenon of Man*. New York: Harper.

———. 1964. *The Future of Man*. New York: Harper & Row.

Tolle, Eckhart. 1999. *The Power of Now: A Guide to Spiritual Enlightenment*. Novato, Calif.: New World Library.

van Vrekhem, Georges. 1998. *Beyond the Human Species: The Life and Work of Sri Aurobindo and the Mother*. St. Paul, Minn.: Paragon House.

Wilber, Ken (ed.). 1984. *Quantum Questions: Mystical Writings of the World's Great Physicists*. Boulder, Colo.: Shambhala.

Wilber, Ken. 1977. *The Spectrum of Consciousness*. Wheaton, Ill.: Theosophical Publishing House.

———. 1995. *Sex, Ecology, Spirituality: The Spirit of Evolution*. Boston: Shambhala.

———. 1996. *The Atman Project*. Wheaton, Ill.: Quest.

———. 1996. *Eye to Eye: The Quest for the New Paradigm*. Boston: Shambhala.

———. 1997. *The Eye of Spirit*. Boston: Shambhala.

———. 1999. *The Marriage of Sense and Soul: Integrating Science and Religion*. New York: Broadway Books.

———. 2000. *A Brief History of Everything*. 2nd revised edition. Boston: Shambhala.

———. 2000. *Integral Psychology*. Boston: Shambhala.

———. 2000. *A Theory of Everything: An Integral Vision for Business, Politics, Science and Spirituality*. Boston: Shambhala.

———. 2001. *No Boundary: Eastern and Western Approaches to Personal Growth*. Boston: Shambhala.

———. 2002. *Boomeritis: A Novel That Will Set You Free*. Boston: Shambhala.

Wills, Garry. 2002. *Why I Am a Catholic*. Boston: Houghton Mifflin.

Yogananda, Paramahansa. 1946. *Autobiography of a Yogi*. Los Angeles: Self-Realization Fellowship.

———. 1975. *Man's Eternal Quest*. Los Angeles: Self-Realization Fellowship.

Index

About the Author

Jim Marion is a rare combination of Christian mystic and public policy lawyer. A Contemporary American mystic who has followed the Christian spiritual path since childhood, Marion spent eight years studying for the priesthood and pursued divinity studies at Hartford Seminary Foundation. After leaving monastic life, he was active in political arenas and received a law degree from Boston University. Since then, Marion has pursued a public policy career in Washington, D.C., where he now lives. Since his pivotal mystical experience as an adolescent, Marion has never ceased to explore the issues, requirements, and challenges of authentic Christian spirituality and inner development. This is his second book for Hampton Roads; the first was *Putting on the Mind of Christ,* published in 2000.

Hampton Roads Publishing Company

. . . for the evolving human spirit

Hampton Roads Publishing Company
publishes books on a variety of subjects,
including metaphysics, health,
visionary fiction, and other related topics.

For a copy of our latest catalog, call toll-free
(800) 766-8009, or send your name and address to:

Hampton Roads Publishing Company, Inc.
1125 Stoney Ridge Road
Charlottesville, VA 22902

e-mail: hrpc@hrpub.com
www.hrpub.com